D1548166

"Creating an amazing customer experience is essential to differentiation. Similarly, peer advisory councils provide recurring, memorable member experiences that will lead to higher member satisfaction and retention. Tina is uniquely qualified to address this concept and does so brilliantly in her excellent new book."

—Dan Gingiss, author of *The Experience Maker* and keynote speaker

"Tina has nailed it! For the last thirty years, being a member of peer groups has been one of the biggest contributors to my success. Tina provides the complete how-to manual for starting, building, and running a world-class peer advisory council."

—Gino Wickman, author of *Traction* and *The EOS Life*

"Entrepreneurial business owners have lonely lives. All actions and decisions in the business will ultimately turn into the entrepreneur's consequence. Peer groups are great resources to reduce the loneliness and increase confidence. However, a peer group without great structure and guidance turns into best-practices sharing. Best practices can be death knells in the fast-moving modern world. *Your Seat at the Table* is the perfect guide to maximizing peer group success and building an entrepreneur's confidence."

—Larry G. Linne, author of *Make the Noise Go Away* and *Leading Performance*

"Tina shows how peer groups can take us beyond the transactional nature of business to create a unique interpersonal community. This book will teach you about how peer advisory councils offer a practical leadership framework where each of us can become more when we work together for everyone."

**—Des McCabe, author of *The Inverted Pyramid of Inclusion*
and chief executive of Diversiton (UK)**

"Tina's powerful methodology is a pillar in GrowthDrive's playbook for building thriving advisory businesses. By helping us deliver sophisticated peer-to-peer support, the wisdom and quick-to-market techniques shared in this book are proving themselves to be ingredients for success—I highly recommend you read and adopt Tina's work."

**—George Sandman, GrowthDrive
CoreValue Advisor Software**

YOUR SEAT AT THE TABLE

YOUR SEAT AT THE TABLE

HOW TO CREATE AND RUN YOUR OWN PEER ADVISORY COUNCIL

TINA CORNER-STOLZ

Forbes | Books

Copyright © 2022 by Tina Corner-Stolz.

All rights reserved. No part of this book may be used or reproduced in any manner whatsoever without prior written consent of the author, except as provided by the United States of America copyright law.

Published by Forbes Books, Charleston, South Carolina.
Member of Advantage Media.

Forbes Books is a registered trademark, and the Forbes Books colophon is a trademark of Forbes Media, LLC.

Printed in the United States of America.

10 9 8 7 6 5 4 3 2 1

ISBN: 979-8-88750-034-8 (Hardcover)
ISBN: 979-8-88750-035-5 (eBook)

LCCN: 2022921653

Cover design by Matthew Morse.
Layout design by Matthew Morse.

This custom publication is intended to provide accurate information and the opinions of the author in regard to the subject matter covered. It is sold with the understanding that the publisher, Forbes Books, is not engaged in rendering legal, financial, or professional services of any kind. If legal advice or other expert assistance is required, the reader is advised to seek the services of a competent professional.

Since 1917, Forbes has remained steadfast in its mission to serve as the defining voice of entrepreneurial capitalism. Forbes Books, launched in 2016 through a partnership with Advantage Media, furthers that aim by helping business and thought leaders bring their stories, passion, and knowledge to the forefront in custom books. Opinions expressed by Forbes Books authors are their own. To be considered for publication, please visit **books.Forbes.com**.

In memory of Arthur Scharff,
my mentor and early visionary
in moderating peer groups

CONTENTS

ACKNOWLEDGMENTS

Because this is my second book, when I first embarked on this project, I was thinking it would be easy to do it all myself. After all, I can do all the writing, I have all the insights, and I have all the answers. I mean, that's why I'm writing the book, right? But we are never alone—even when we're "at the top." This book was truly a team effort by so many people, and thanking them on this page seems minor compared to the major impact they've made.

First, to my beloved parents, Fran and Joe. They were the ultimate role models for me on the value of relationships and partnerships. It was their influence that gave me the foundation for my peer group model. Their wisdom and love continue to guide me to this day, even though they're gone.

To my husband, Scott. Big hugs for being my biggest cheerleader and my own personal advisory board member. You are my safe haven, providing wise advice and triple-checking my thought process while alleviating all my doubts.

To Mary Martin, whose understanding of what I do helped bring clarity to these pages. Your magic made my concepts and writing more professional and clearer, and you challenged my thinking at times, which I so appreciated. I miss working with you every day, as you made it a joy to go on this journey together. You are the consummate professional.

To my core team, Tiffany Brandt and Monica Peverini, for your excitement about the book and what it means to us as a team and the industry. You protected my time so I could meet deadlines and kept the company initiatives moving forward without skipping a beat.

To Monique Higginbotham, another core team member, for your design brilliance in creating the diagrams and resources that complete the narrative of this book. Your talent continues to amaze me.

To Des McCabe, thank you for your coaching and wisdom regarding structuring our academy and community. You are the community expert who has guided us in creating something special.

To my publisher, Forbes Books. You assembled an excellent team of diverse experts with Laura Rashley, Kristin Hackler, Matthew Morse, and Henry Clougherty, who advised me, supported me, and gave me peace of mind. The book framework was in good hands. A particular callout to Dee Kerr for your enthusiasm, commitment, and chicken lights providing "aha" moments for all (you know what I mean).

To all Licensed Partners and moderators whom I work with today and with whom I have worked, this book is a result of all the conversations, successes, and missteps from our journey together. It's your questions, your ideas, and your inquisitive mindsets that motivated the words on these pages. I thank you for your innovative ideas that push this industry forward, your better practices that happen every day, and your desire to be the best. You push me to new levels. I love working with and appreciate every one of you.

To all my colleagues in the industry, thank you for doing what you do. Your role is so important in providing a way for entrepreneurs, companies, and leaders to positively impact not just themselves but also their companies, their employees, and ultimately, their communities. You are the caretakers of this industry. And my hope is that this book helps take care of you.

To you, the reader, I'm grateful for your interest in peer groups, for your desire to continuously be a learner of this profession, and for spending your time with me. And to those of you who have tried to launch a group and failed or are struggling to maintain, keep positive. This book is for you.

And last, to God for putting in my heart the desire to change how peer groups are thought of, run, and created. I hope I listened well.

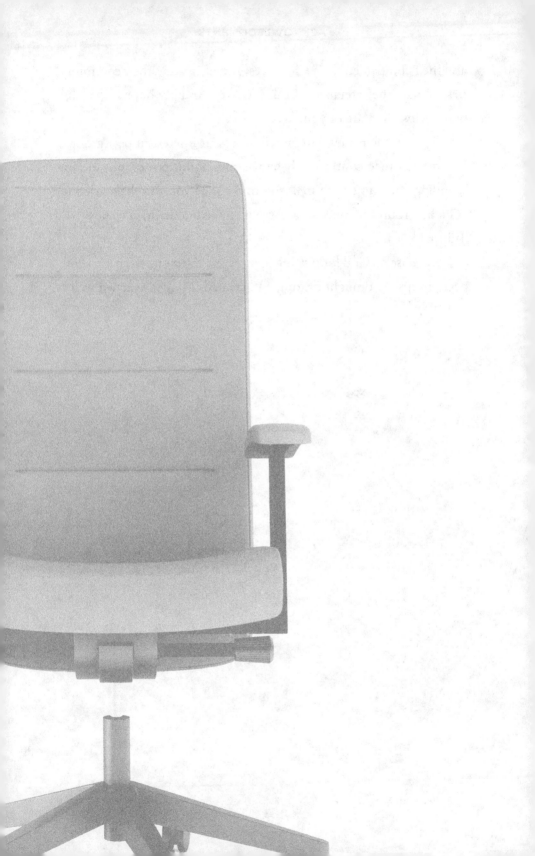

INTRODUCTION

I've created, developed, moderated, and mentored over one thousand unique peer advisory council (PaC) meetings and have devoted over seventeen years and over twenty thousand hours to this work. *Why?* Because I, too, am a business owner in the peer group space. I know what it's like to feel alone running peer groups, to wonder whether you'll ever get a new group off the ground, and to make decisions about new members, old members, and business tactics you have no experience with. I've walked in your shoes and know that the path is often bumpy at best, with no road map to guide you and no way to know which bumps are OK and which are problematic.

If you're reading this book, you likely

- want to start a peer group and maximize your chances for success,
- have had a peer group fall apart or only partially succeed,
- are already running a group and want to be the best at it, and
- want a heads-up about all of the ways things can go sideways and how to handle them.

How Did I Get Here?

My dad was a small business entrepreneur, and I had no intention of following the same path. I thought corporate life was my path, and I tried it and excelled. But you know what they say about the apple and the tree. Watching Dad succeed as an entrepreneur and watching *how* he succeeded left such a profound impression on me that I felt pulled toward following in his footsteps.

We lived in a rural community in the Midwest, where everyone either was a farmer or worked for one. Although we had a farm, Dad also had a diverse range of small businesses—a car dealership, a liquor store, and an oil company, all in the nearest small town. At one point, he was running all of them. I have no idea how! His last business was selling used concrete mixers worldwide. When he passed in his early eighties in 2012, his colleagues told me he was known for reinventing the used concrete mixer industry, but more important, he was known for the relationships he had with his peers. And they cherished those relationships. I knew my dad valued them as well because he was always telling funny or poignant stories about his peers and employees. And when I worked for him during high school and college, I got to see how he cared for people. He spent time nurturing relationships—cultivating them. He cared deeply for those he loved, and it showed.

My formal sales education began with a salesmanship class at the University of Missouri. I barely skated through with less-than-stellar marks. It seems that my answers, based on the way my father ran his businesses, weren't what the instructor wanted. They wanted me to focus on finances and transactions, but I gave them answers based on relationships. This was when I felt the full impact of that old saying "Experience trumps academics." Learning from others who've been there and done that has enormous value. They've paved the way, taken the hard knocks, and shouldered the burden so things might be easier for those who follow them. That's what I want to do for you; I want to pave the way.

I've watched so many of my peers fail at launching their own peer groups or struggle to keep them together or grow once they had some success. They were working really hard, but hard wasn't working. I was working really hard, too, and it *was* working. *Why?* Because I understood the value of what Dad would call relationships, but they were more than that; they were Strategic Partnerships.

> I understood the value of what Dad would call relationships, but they were more than that; they were Strategic Partnerships.

When I was growing up on the farm, at one point Dad partnered with a fellow farmer, sharing equipment and labor, helping each other save a levee from breaking that otherwise would have flooded all our crops. I'm sure there were other things I wasn't aware of. As I got older, I saw him partner with other farmers to make deals happen and even with his next-door neighbor when Dad granted him an easement. All of this partnering was with people in a similar position—peers—and each partnership was sealed with a handshake.

It's not as though I was documenting this or even knew the details of everything that was happening. I was absorbing this idea of smart partnering, and I internalized it; it became who I was. Partnering was effective, made life easier, and created deeper relationships that were more fun and engaging. It gave me an edge—a secret weapon. But more important, sharing goals with peers almost guaranteed success because there was more than one person motivated to make them happen.

It makes sense, then, that during my early career years with a global telecom company, I worked partnerships into my position. I started in outside sales, and in eleven years, I had advanced my way up to running a $1.2B North American telecom division. It was there that I created the most successful partner model in the industry, earning me a spot on the Most Influential in Telecom list. I always thought of my success as shared because it would have never happened without my Strategic Partners, whom I valued as teammates.

Even with all the accolades, true entrepreneurship was nagging at me. I wanted something different, but I didn't know exactly what it would look like. First, I went the start-up route for about two years, which went fairly well until 9/11, at which point I left, and it continued on to become an IPO without me. But I wasn't happy anyway; that model wasn't fulfilling to me.

Soon afterward, as I was driving through Washington, DC, one Sunday morning, running ahead of schedule for an event, I drove by the conference center. There was a franchise expo going on, and I figured, *Why not?* and stopped. I had only thirty minutes. I barreled in, looked for a map of the franchises that were business oriented, and briefly checked them all out but didn't find them compelling. As I was zipping down the last aisle toward the exit, someone from a "peer advisory franchise" stopped me in my tracks to talk to me. That was the beginning. Two months later, I bought a peer advisory group franchise. It was a fluke that changed the course of my career; I had found the intersection of partnering and working with small businesses. And I loved it.

When I launched my franchise, I naturally assumed I needed a partnership, even though it wasn't part of the franchise's business model. My assumption was correct. I believe my partnerships were the sole reason my launch was the most successful one they ever had.

On Wall Street, TINA is an acronym for "There is no alternative." After observing so many franchisees fail as well as entrepreneurs going it on their own, I realized the peer advisory business isn't like *Field of Dreams*. If you build it, there's no guarantee that anyone's coming. There is no alternative: when it comes to PaCs, you cannot grow your business without partnerships. I knew this; it was the secret sauce as to why so many PaCs failed, and I set out to prove that there was an alternative—and better—option to the traditional model. So I sold my franchise and set out to build a new model based on what I had learned—and experienced—were the keys to success at launching groups. It was time for me to reinvent, to be innovative, just like my dad. I created the peer advisory council (PaC), and this book and my training academy were born.

The Structure of This Book

I've organized this book in the way I teach the course it's based on, which is the way I wish someone had taught me: from the beginning. We'll begin with my philosophy of excellence, clarity, and process—everything you need to know to deliver a flawless customer experience for the members of your PaC. If that happens, your PaC is a success. I'll guide you through designing everything from a prospect's first encounter with you to transforming that person into a lifelong member who continues to find value in your PaC and becomes your champion. That's what I'm doing with this book—providing a road map from your idea to its impeccable execution. And when you have impeccable execution, you've created cheerleaders. You've created fans and evangelists who will tell their friends.

Rinse and repeat.

Chapter 1, "The What and Why of Peer Advisory Council (PaC) Moderating," sets the stage by defining critical terms and making sure we have a shared language. If there's one thing I've learned over twenty years, it's that you need to be on the same page with people when you talk about this. It's not like anyone is wrong about anything; it's that there are different interpretations of words and even some entirely different terminology, and sometimes it's unclear what the jargon is referring to.

Once the shared language is clear, we'll get into the foundation of your PaC as a business. What's your idea? What field will you establish yourself in?

Chapter 2, "Identifying Your Peer Advisory Council," will guide you through identifying the idea that has the highest likelihood of success for you. I encourage you to have an open mind here. Most entrepreneurs aren't aware of how many groups are possible, how varied they are, and how many new types are popping up every day. What's the right type for you? And how can you capitalize on your passion to lead a group that aligns with this passion?

Chapter 3, "A Step-by-Step Guide to Assembling a Successful PaC," discusses the nuances of putting a group together, like how to build partnerships that will help you find your ideal prospect and how to put true peers together with intention rather than tossing people together because they have similar numbers of employees or similar revenue. There's much more to it, and this is the first step to launching successfully.

Chapter 4, "Designing the Initial Experience," explains what happens between signing your first member and holding your first meeting. You'll learn how to create a customized experience for the new member from the beginning. This chapter includes what you should have begun to decide prior to the first meeting as well as what you should be preparing for new members.

Chapter 5, "The Formula for Successful Meetings," reveals the four consecutive steps that ensure value for your members at every meeting. I'll discuss the Why and the How for each step as well as the importance of an intentional agenda.

Chapter 6 ("What Does It Mean to Be a Moderator?") describes what moderating is and isn't. I talk about the soft skills necessary and the mindset you have to have, and I lay out the moderator's code of conduct.

Chapter 7, "The Moderator's Journey," will help you discover what you don't know you don't know about your journey to launching and moderating. It can be exhilarating one moment and humbling the next. How do you know you're doing a good job—or even a great job?

Chapter 8 ("Retaining Groups and Members Long Term") will take you through techniques to help you transform members of a group into lifelong clients. Minimizing turnover by looking out for red flags and having systems in place to maintain engagement sets you up for your highest ROI.

Chapter 9, "Before You Sell One Membership," describes the many decision points during your journey as a PaC business owner. I'll provide the questions you need to ask yourself as well as better practices for various decisions and situations.

Finally, the conclusion presents my final insights and messages for you. I hope you're able to see that underneath all the structure and processes are my deep love for this work and my commitment to creating environments conducive to *ahas* and the cultivation of lifelong, supportive relationships.

At the end of every chapter, you'll find a brief outline of the chapter's key takeaways along with a list of resources that will enable you to put key concepts into practice. To access those resources, please see the QR code at the back of the book in the "Want to Start Your Journey Now?" section to be directed to these exclusive materials on my website.

Building and successfully moderating a peer advisory council is about building a dream team. This book is for the dream team visionaries and architects, those who aspire to work with their ideal clients and have a passion to see them succeed. You are the North Star pilots. I offer you this comprehensive flight plan to help you navigate the journey to professional enlightenment in every kind of weather.

CHAPTER 1

The What and Why of Peer Advisory Council (PaC) Moderating

I wanted to have a special dining experience on this trip. After all, fifty is a pretty big deal. And if singular dining experiences are your thing, you might know that the French Laundry in Yountville, California is the place to be. It's a Michelin three-star restaurant owned by renowned chef Thomas Keller; it's been ranked the number-one restaurant in the United States, and it was called "the best restaurant in the world, period" by the late Anthony Bourdain.

The French Laundry is known worldwide for its menu, service, and exclusivity. Dining there says that you won't settle for anything but excellence and you trust that the establishment will deliver. The chef chooses what you'll eat and changes the menu daily. You choose either the standard "tasting menu" or the vegetable-based one; it's a minimum of $350 per person, paid in advance, and no, that doesn't include fabulous Napa wine or add-ons such as a quail egg or slice of Kobe beef.

Even their reservation protocol speaks to their standards and the environment they're creating. The expression of exclusivity, quality, and uniqueness of experience generates an amount of demand that will always outstrip the supply of available seating. I was actually nervous when I called for a reservation almost a year in advance (they currently only take reservations one month in advance). This was an important event, and I needed to find out what I didn't know I didn't know. I was told that the only reservation even close to the date I wanted was for lunch and to allow four hours. I was shocked.

What? Not only is this going to cost a small fortune, but also … four hours for lunch? How can I spare four hours when there's so much to do in the Napa area? I'll miss the whole day—the whole afternoon of wine tasting I already felt I didn't have enough time for!

My reaction instantly reminded me of the most-voiced objection to joining a peer advisory group of any kind: "I don't have time for a four-hour meeting; I'm too busy running my business." I didn't think I had time for a four-hour lunch, but I wanted the experience. I had to trust that it would be worth my time and my money. And it exceeded my expectations immensely. So much that here I am, years later, still talking about it. What if you could create that kind of demand and experience for your peer groups?

What if your groups were thought of as exclusive, for which prospects had to wait for an opening? My formula for peer advisory councils (PaCs) can make that happen for you.

Let's see what else happened at the French Laundry …

Silently he prepared me for what to expect next. He took my plate, knowing I was finished and without me noticing. Then I realized my glass had been replaced with a different wine to accompany the new course I had been given. How had that happened? *When* had it happened? How had he anticipated what I wanted? Needed! The servers were flawless, silent, and ghostlike. It was amazing to be on the receiving end of such a display of art and science woven beautifully together to create the ultimate customer experience.

This is how members should feel after their peer advisory council meetings. Believe it or not, designing and delivering a fine dining experience isn't all that different from designing and delivering a PaC meeting. What if you moderated groups so effectively and the value was so extraordinary that members didn't blink at the time and money they were spending with you? What if they treasured that time instead?

After that meal I was struck by all the ways in which quality is quality, regardless of the industry and the type of experience you're creating for your customers. And if you want to create the highest-quality experience, you need to make sure that no detail is overlooked and that each step of your process is designed and executed with intention and excellence. That includes the very first moment of contact.

> **What if you moderated groups so effectively and the value was so extraordinary that members didn't blink at the time and money they were spending with you?**

How do you approach prospects or get them to approach you? How do you prepare them for a meeting they'll look forward to, not one they dread they might be "sold" to? The moment they say yes to joining your group, how do you create a stress-free entry into the group? How do you launch a new group? How do you orchestrate an effective introduction of a new member to existing members? What's the experience of existing members being positioned to accept the new member, and how can each meeting be full of *aha* moments you're responsible for moderating?

Each meeting should be a remarkable customer experience, not a meeting left to chance based on who's there and what they bring to the meeting. In the model I created and teach in my Peer Advisory Council Academy, the moderator is akin to Thomas Keller, who creates the menu and is ultimately responsible for the outcome, regardless of who shows up for lunch or dinner. Successful moderators don't sit back and let the members decide what will happen and when. Instead, we use a structure and build on a foundation that has been proven successful. Integral to the success of that structure is that it allows for the uncertainty that inevitably occurs, and it provides a skillful way to pivot the agenda to accommodate. This creates an exceptional experience for members, who won't even notice there was a situation that could have gone sideways. A skillful moderator makes everything that happens look like it was supposed to happen.

I was never taught how to do this when I entered the industry. Nor was I taught how to effectively put a group together or how to moderate a meeting. I was taught how to market and how to put an agenda together—that's it. There was no talk of the mingling of art and science. Most important, no one told me that moderating was much more than "running a meeting" or that the moderator's

> **Great moderating isn't noticed, but bad moderating is.**

skill is pivotal to the member experience. Members leave if the moderator is bad, but they also stay because the moderator is good. They think they're staying because of the other members, and they are. But they notice how wonderful and helpful the other members are because of the skill of the moderator. Great moderating isn't noticed, but bad moderating is. Furthermore, in successful groups it might look like the group came together randomly and magically achieved chemistry. But what's unnoticed again is that the moderator assembled that group strategically. That group launched and connected because someone knew what they were doing when they designed the experience.

Important: This is not an instructional guide for running meetings.

There are plenty of books about running meetings—that's not what this is. This book is specifically for people who want to be in the business of moderating peer advisory council (PaC) meetings. "Peer advisory council" is what I call groups composed of true peers in the business world who come together to work on their challenges, opportunities, problems, and ideas. Because they are true peers, they're uniquely positioned to help one another. You may or may not have heard of meetings like this, and you might be thinking they're similar to Mastermind meetings. It's easy to see why you'd think that, but there's a big difference that we'll get more into later. For now, know that the primary difference between the PaC and other peer group models is the presence of—and the significance of—a moderator. The moderator in the PaC model is actually the business owner. They are in the business of assembling and moderating PaC meetings.

My most shocking observation (there is no public data) as a franchisee with a company that runs peer groups is that the failure rate is incredibly high: more than 50 percent. And from all my conversations and watching attempted launches in various markets across the country for nearly twenty years, it was clear that the deciding factor in the success of peer groups is the skill of the moderator. Whether we're talking about turnover of members within groups, which can be devastating (even when a group is assembled correctly), or difficulty launching, or absenteeism, the outcome is almost completely dependent on how the moderator handles the situation. There simply hasn't been enough of the right kind of training for moderators. Until now.

When the moderator of a peer advisory council is at their best, the members aren't aware that every detail has been thoughtfully choreographed. Great moderating skills make it look spontaneous and effortless, despite the strategy underpinning every move. Like the French Laundry demonstrated so flawlessly, the moderator profession is complex and multilayered. It takes a commitment to lifelong learning to perfect. It's a function of knowledge plus time practicing. You can speed up your intake of knowledge, but there's no shortcut to practice—to developing experience. The only way to deepen and broaden your experience and hone your skills is to train yourself (or to get some training!) and get started with the practice of moderating peer groups.

You might be thinking: If the failure rate is so high, why would I entertain the thought of running my own PaC? Because there is now a formula that addresses the causes of most failures. If you find it enjoyable to interact with people who want to better their businesses and achieve impressive missions and visions, and you want to be instrumental in guiding them in coping with challenges and opportunities, there's no more rewarding way to spend your time. You'll be paid handsomely for your skill at moderating and earn a high return on your time. Plus, you'll have the flexibility of running your own business.

Welcome to the Wild West!

Your Seat at the Table is a stand-alone description of the fundamentals of creating, launching, and moderating successful PaCs. And although you could skip around to the chapters most appealing or urgent to you, I highly recommend reading all of them because the success of the model depends on your understanding of the terminology and the context I'll provide. This field is still in the Wild West stage. The terminology isn't universally understood or agreed upon, there's no regulatory body, and the public—including potential moderators—is justifiably confused.

I'll begin at the beginning, defining the terms I'll be using throughout the book. This ensures we're on the same page as we move through each step of the process.

The Peer Advisory Council (PaC)

Peer groups have been around for thousands of years, come in many forms, and come together in different ways. Not all of them are in the service of commerce, and not all of them are in the service of advice exchange or mutual professional development. Here are some groups or types of groups throughout history that have peer-group elements to them. See whether you can notice what they all have in common.

- If you look back to ancient Greece, you'll find that the greatest teachers (e.g., Plato, Aristotle, Socrates, and later the Stoics) sought out and surrounded themselves with others who would keep their minds sharp and challenge their thinking. In fact, the Socratic method, used in many educational institutions today, is a model for helping students dig deeper and deeper into their own thoughts to find answers for themselves. What makes the Socratic method different from other styles of teaching is that the teacher's job isn't to provide the answers but to ask the right questions and cultivate skillful habits of thinking in their students.

- Jesus's disciples are considered a peer group, and as a way of continuing that tradition, many Christian churches have peer groups called discipleships. These groups gather in the same vein and are connected not only by their shared faith but also by their commitment to advise each other and be sounding boards for each other.

- Perhaps the most famous peer group was King Arthur's Round Table in the twelfth century. The significance of the shape of the table was that no knight could claim he was more important than the others, as there was no head of the table. Equality was built in, although there were rules for some seats. For instance, one was to remain vacant, as it was reserved for whoever was successful in his quest for the Holy Grail. These days, we have roundtable discussions in which peers (who are frequently experts) gather to discuss a particular topic, and all have equal time to speak. No vacant seats required!

- In the United States, our forefathers had "cabinets" of advisors to guide and support them. In 1727, the first official peer group in what would become the United States was formed by Ben Franklin and called the Junto Group. Its objective was to promote useful knowledge. It had twelve members (including a chemist, physician, botanist, mathematician, engineer, geographer, cabinetmaker, bartender, clerk, printer, and surveyor), and it met weekly and lasted thirty-eight years. In 1901, President Theodore Roosevelt continued the peer-group tradition when he took office at the age of forty-two. And in 1921, while Warren G. Harding was president, he was part of a peer group called the Vagabonds, which included Thomas Edison, Henry Ford, and Harvey Firestone. The idea of the cabinet continues to this day in America, although the president appoints the members, and their positions have more to do with the enforcement of laws than advising.

- *Communities of Practice* are groups that come together organically inside a company or an industry and are composed of professionals with the same expertise and an intention to share knowledge and best practices or solve problems in their work or industry. The members aren't required to participate, the meetings are informal, and the entire project is self-organizing. This isn't a business model; attendance varies, and that's fine. And topics discussed are sometimes personal or otherwise not work related. Maybe there's a facilitator or leader for a particular meeting, and maybe it's more freestyle. Either way, it's not a moneymaking venture; that's not the intention.

- American industrialist Andrew Carnegie, who amassed a fortune in the steel industry, had a *Master Mind* (he used two words) group. In *Think and Grow Rich,* Napoleon Hill describes the fifty-man (and yes, they were all men) group as providing Carnegie with advice and counsel. After discussing the topic with Carnegie, Hill wrote, "The coordination of knowledge and effort between two or more people who work towards a definite purpose in a spirit of harmony ... no two minds ever come together without thereby creating a third, invisible intangible force, which may be likened to a third mind." This was the original intention of the Mastermind (which is now one word), and you'll see that similar to the cabinet of our forefathers, the concept has not changed.

Meanwhile, there are also groups of peers that gather for social reasons or political reasons—not to mention that there are networking groups of peers. For these reasons and others, I'm intentionally using the phrase *peer advisory council,* or *PaC.* Simply put, not all peer groups have an advisory element or consider all members of equal status. Finally, not all peer groups are assembled to create knowledge or best practices or ideas for increasing or expanding *business*. Peer advisory councils have business at their center.

A Word about Mastermind Groups

Mastermind groups have become fashionable in the last few decades, and their structure and definition seem to have strayed from Hill's 1937 description. Just as with "cabinet" and "roundtable" (and frankly, thousands of other words), language evolves and sometimes gets messy. This is one of those times, and my advice is simply to ask someone what they mean if you aren't sure. Some people use Mastermind the same way as I use peer advisory council, and some people don't. I've seen three versions of Mastermind groups, but again, keep in mind that some Mastermind groups define themselves the same way I define peer advisory councils.

First, some Masterminds are assembled by business owners who invite their clients to gather with the purpose of advancing programs they've developed. They use the gatherings as ways to leverage the support of their clients or students. Many times, this type of Mastermind is an extension of an initial program, requiring some kind of fee or change in level of membership. This creates an additional revenue stream in exchange for the assumed value of gathering with others who have the same designation or other professional interest.

On the other hand, some business owners invite their clients to gather, and there's no fee. In this scenario, the group is a way to continue the client relationship and an opportunity for members to practice what they learned from the business owner's program. This has elements of a Community of Practice, as there will be reflection, feedback, and discussion, but it's likely more structured. The business owner isn't necessarily part of each meeting but might pop in every now and then to answer questions or advise. Either way, the business owner is the expert.

Finally, there are groups built around the people leading them, who are subject matter experts. In this case, members may have varied backgrounds, different careers, and nothing in common other than wanting to learn more about the topic the leader is an expert in. In other words, they join to learn more from the "master."

Net message? Mastermind groups often have leaders whose mastery of a given topic is the focus. The members are there to learn from that person, the discussion is narrow and confined to the topic and the practices around the topic, and the leader clearly directs the discussion to optimize the transmission of their knowledge to the group. This might seem obvious, but it needs to be said—the primary goal is not for the members to learn from one another (although that will presumably happen) but for them to learn from the "master."

Peer advisory councils, on the other hand, are composed of people with a shared interest and purpose *who have similar levels of experience or knowledge*, and they're there to share what they know and to learn from each other. There is no master. And whether their focus is on how to be smarter, do something better, make more money, or make wiser decisions, *they have a similar level of sophistication.* So while their experiences will vary, and they expect that, it's important for them to feel like they're with peers they can learn from. *That perception is key.* Why? Because then they believe they can contribute to the success of others by sharing their own experiences and insights. The result? Feedback derived and confidence gained from their peer advisory council meetings help members advance exponentially. This enables the group experience to be a force multiplier that regularly leads members to *aha* moments of clarity.

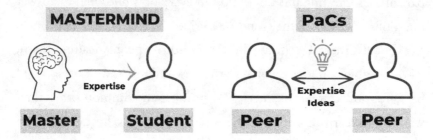

Moderators versus Facilitators

Having a trusted, unbiased group of peers you know will maintain confidentiality and not judge you allows you to be vulnerable to learn and grow. But this growth doesn't necessarily just happen on its own; it needs cultivation. And for that, the group should have a moderator. Think about televised political debates. The person who runs the debate is called a moderator, not a facilitator. *Why?* Because they're knowledgeable about those participating and the topics raised, they look for insights and opinions to be teased out or highlighted, and they make sure everyone participates.

Moderators of PaCs aren't there to move through agendas; they're there to create experiences for their members. They're architects who choose the members, set the agendas, and preside over the discussions. They're knowledgeable about the type of group they're leading, they engage members to participate equally, they monitor group dynamics, and they drive the meeting toward insights for members.

> A moderator is someone whose presence within the group is acknowledged by the group and whose actions are mostly transparent to the group.

I'll spend more time discussing this in chapter 6 ("What Does

It Mean to Be a Moderator?"), but for now, know that a moderator is someone whose presence within the group is acknowledged by the group and whose actions are mostly transparent to the group. The members understand that the moderator guides, nudges, and moves the meeting along as well as directs them to dive deeper into certain topics. The members know that the moderator knows when and how to encourage dialogue and when and how to gently direct the group's dialogue toward leadership growth and personal learning. The moderator knows most of the answers but pushes the members to support their peers instead.

• • •

Now that we're on the same page with language, let's talk about the various options for creating a PaC and what's best for you.

 Takeaways

- Moderating is a profession that requires skill and training.
- The obstacle to successfully launching a group is the lack of complete training.
- Universal terminology doesn't exist yet.
- Peer advisory council (PaC) members don't learn from the moderator; they learn from their peers.

Resources

- The Predicator Assessment. Scan the QR code at the back of the book to take a short quiz to see if starting a PaC is the right fit for you.

CEOs from various industries
Local + In person

Business owners from similar industries
National + Virtual

Presidents of large marinas
National + Hybrid

Senior Leaders at Family Firms
Local + In person

Female Executives
Local + In person

Faith-Based Entrepreneurs
Local + In person

CHROs from Healthcare companies with over 1,000 employees
Global + Hybrid

CFOs from Global companies aspiring to do business in one
foreign country
Global + Virtual

Leaders from within the same company
Local or National + In person or Hybrid

Manufacturing Clients of an Accounting Firm
Regional + Virtual

CHAPTER 2

Identifying Your Peer Advisory Council

What you just read are all examples of business PaCs from traditional (top) to newer structures (bottom), and I promise you there are new types popping up everyday. Part of the intention of this chapter is to expand your thinking beyond traditional types of groups. This field has the opportunity to become more personalized and niche driven. It's happening now on a small scale, in pockets. But make no mistake: there's so much more to this field than PaCs built around traditional CEOs (although they remain the most popular types), and I'd like to help you find your niche. How can you capitalize on your passion by creating, launching, and moderating a group around that passion? And once you've figured that out, how will you deliver your PaCs? Virtually? In person? Both? Let's work through these important details together.

Answer This Question First

Do you already know what type of peer advisory council you want to moderate? Or maybe you're already moderating today and you want to expand your business. Have you identified the intersection of where your passion lies, where your expertise can be most helpful, and where you have the most connections? If you think you know, take a gander at this cautionary tale from my training academy.

Jim wanted to launch a PaC that consisted of construction-related business owners only. His father had worked for a general contractor for most of his life, and Jim thought, "Why not? I know something about the construction industry from listening to my dad talk about work at the dinner table. Plus, it would be nice to be able to have something in common with him, and we could chat about it when I visit. He's retired now, and I'm sure he'd get a kick out of me doing this and would love to hear about the industry he loved so much."

Sounds good so far. What could go wrong?

Jim embarked on creating his construction-themed PaC of business owners and intended to meet in person locally. He was excited and wanted to surprise his dad and tell him about it, but he wanted to secure his first few members. To that end, Jim made a list of all the general contractors (GCs) in the area as well as the related construction firms, such as plumbing, electrical, concrete, roofing, architecture, etc., and then targeted the most prestigious firm in each category. He planned what he would say when he called, describing why his council would be unique. He was eager to start, and no one else appeared to be in this space—at least, no one he could find.

Note: If no one else has done it, it's either brilliant and you need to pursue it, or others have tried it, only to discover how problematic it was and abandon their efforts (hopefully in favor of something else).

Jim prioritized calling GCs first, figuring that if he signed one as the anchor member, all the other calls to tradesmen would be easier. After his call to the first GC was a success and he had his first member, Jim thought, "Wow, this is easy!" However, secretly he wondered why, and he soon found his answer.

He began calling the tradesmen next, and his first two calls were rejections, causing him to rethink his strategy. What exactly had happened? Jim failed to consider that a general contractor shouldn't be in a group of tradesmen because GCs hire them as subcontractors. Or sometimes the GC competes with them directly. In other words, his PaC seemed to have a conflict of interest designed into it. He thought a GC would be complementary to tradespeople, but that's not how it works in real life—at least not from the perspective of the tradespeople. The GC was keen on joining his group because he saw an opportunity to gather intel from the trades, and they could be potential clients. This was a great networking opportunity for the GC, but Jim's PaC wasn't supposed to be a networking group.

The GC wasn't on equal footing with the tradespeople, and Jim thought he had to start all over. Not only that, but he'd have to call his first member—the GC—and tell him he couldn't be in the PaC. He looked like he didn't know what he was doing. He sure didn't want to make that call.

This is when I met Jim, and we brainstormed how to right the ship that had sailed. All hope was not lost. After Jim learned how to think through ideas thoroughly and critically, looking for all of the holes and barriers *before* making any calls, he realized his PaC wasn't a bad idea. This was a case of not taking the time to think about what it would be like from the perspectives of the members of the group. That's a nuance that can make or break an idea. Jim figured out he could have saved time, money, and embarrassment and been able to accomplish his dream of assembling the right-fit members for his themed PaC. In fact, he could still do it. *How?*

General contractors are competitors of each other if they operate in the same geographical area, as they might bid on the same jobs, using the same subcontractors and resources. They can benefit from being in a PaC with other GCs, but they have to be geographically noncompetitive. So Jim assembled a virtual group of GCs in other locations. He could also put his trade niche PaC together, but it would have to be without GCs.

Thinking through the nuances of any niche PaC you're considering prior to initiating that first contact is crucial to your success!

Thinking through the nuances of any niche PaC you're considering prior to initiating that first contact is crucial to your success! The last thing you want is to launch a group and find a conflict or a major gap that inhibits full participation because you have the wrong member or members involved.

The Seven Most Common Categories of PaCs

I've been doing this for almost two decades, and there are five categories of peer advisory councils I've watched succeed over and over again and two new emerging ones that have a lot of promise. There are likely other ones, but if you like the idea of moderating PaCs and you have a lot of interests, or you haven't landed on a single topic that thrills you more than others, perhaps this will narrow down your thinking.

The intention here is to point out where your passion and expertise show up. If you answer *no* to any of the questions, that's an indication that the category might not be the best fit for you. However if your answer is *no* and you're nevertheless interested in the category, ask yourself what you can do to acquire expertise or knowledge to turn your *no* into a *yes*.

Position, Title, Level of Responsibility

Members: CEOs, business owners, presidents, CFOs, senior leaders, executives, CIOs, CHROs, etc.

Decision points:

- Do you love working with leaders of a specific type?
- Do you have experience as one of these leaders, or have you worked / do you work with them?

Advantages:

- This category can include all industries, which means there's a broader market to pull from.
- Pursuing leaders as group members tends to be a relatively easy sell because they make the decisions or have budget or profit-and-loss responsibility.
- This is the most common and well-known category. Most people come to it already understanding it because they've heard about it or know people who have participated in these PaCs.
- Members have a tendency to easily think they're with true peers because they have the same title. While this isn't true, their belief makes it easy for them to join.

Disadvantages:

- Differentiating yourself is critical to succeeding among the competition *because* this is the most common PaC. You can do this with a different agenda, tools, and your expertise. If you thoroughly think through these components, there's no disadvantage.
- Matching members by title only isn't sufficient and doesn't result in a group of true peers. We'll do a deep dive on how to do this in the next chapter, "A Step-by-Step Guide to Assembling a Successful PaC."

1. Industry Specific

Members: Operate in a specific industry (e.g., marine, manufacturing, technology, construction, accounting, law), and there's no conflict between or among the industries represented.

Decision points:

- Do you understand something about the industry?
- Do you know the lingo, the common challenges, the pitfalls, and the trends?
- Are there industry levels to consider (e.g., marine 2020 or auto 2020)?
- Does geography matter? Considering geography is necessary to avoid conflicts of interest. Geography doesn't always matter, but it matters enough to at least ask the question.

Advantages:

- Shared lingo, industry terms, contacts, and customers. This category reduces the need to educate members on industry nuances.
- Shared financial data or metrics can lend to true benchmarking.
- Industry trend analyses, discussion, and observations are relatable to all and can lend more insights to the group than if observed independently.
- The level of conversation can be more specific and targeted and many times more effective and valuable. For example, conversations around bonding or working with subcontractors or project management can be exponentially helpful because everyone will have stories and lessons learned to contribute.

- Members don't have to reinvent the wheel, as there's frequently someone who has done and maybe even perfected what others are thinking about doing.

- Industry knowledge, resources, and connections are shared. There's a higher level of opportunity to help each other leverage specific knowledge that directly has an impact on the others. Examples: "We use this specific project management software and not the others because of *xyz*," or "I know someone who might be a good fit for your job opening," or "I know of a project being released for bid."

Disadvantages:

- Groupthink can emerge. For example, when the council accepts "It's the way it is" for common challenges or ways of doing business, members are saying they don't believe there's a solution, so they should just accept it, work around it, or ignore it—whatever *it* is. This is a mindset that says, "Since it's a problem for everyone and has been forever, there must not be a different solution." Groupthink occurs when there's no creative thinking, no innovations considered that could disrupt the status quo.

- One way to counteract groupthink of any kind is to make sure you have a full PaC that includes diversity in thinking. Keeping groups small is an invitation to groupthink and an obstacle to reaching deeper levels. At the same time, finding sufficient members to craft a full, diverse group can be difficult if your industry is already narrow or if you're meeting in person and geography is challenging. For example, one of our Licensed Partner manufacturer groups diversified by combining high-tech companies that use robotics with traditional, more labor-intensive companies.

- After a period of time, meetings can get stale because of the wealth of commonality. Bringing in new ideas, changing up the format, and pushing the envelope on performance will help keep things fresh.

2. Geography

Members: They all operate in a specific geography. For example, they all operate globally, have global interests, have specific challenges operating globally or gaining entry into a specific country, or they want to expand globally.

Decision points:

- Do you have a broad understanding of the geography or global nuances, such as language barriers, culture differences, and business-practice differences?
- Are you open to doing virtual meetings all the time or sometimes to accommodate traveling members or members in different time zones?

Advantages:

- PaCs created around geography can be powerful groups that create change beyond their own organizations. They can create global change or directly impact a country, such as a PaC that wants to learn to do business in Africa to impact health conditions there. They share that common cause and mission.
- Usually this category is directly aligned with strategic initiatives inside the organization making the PaC a part of their

strategy. For example, a global organization has specific environmental, social, and governance (ESG) initiatives, and being with a group that has similar ESG initiatives is beneficial. One result is long-term members for you.

- You have an opportunity for the members to be Resource Connectors for each other. Being a Resource Connector is essentially being someone who can refer or provide resources when a fellow member needs someone. It's the person who answers when someone says, "I need to find someone who can ..." This is discussed at greater length in chapters 4 and 9.

Disadvantages:

- When you're global, you have members in many time zones, and that makes it hard to find one time to meet that's convenient for everyone.
- Getting the members to truly bond and be vulnerable can be challenging, as there might be cultural differences around how intimate professionals should be with one another.

3. Specialty

Members: Woman-owned businesses, Family Firms, women in technology, investors, religious groups, exit-planning-focused or succession-focused leaders, people looking to discuss fast growth, etc.

Decision points:

- You have a direct connection to the specialty, either through belief, experience, or knowledge.
- You have an affinity for helping this type of member succeed.

Advantages:

- It can be very rewarding to work, as you share something important to you with all of the members. The bond is stronger than with other groups.
- You're exposed to conversations around topics important to you that only certain types of people will understand. For example, a single parent running a business and trying to balance both critical responsibilities of home and boss wouldn't get great insight from members who aren't balancing the same priorities.

Disadvantages:

- Tunnel vision can occur when discussing challenges or opportunities that don't take into consideration the real world of business. For example, women-only groups whose clients, vendors, or competitors include men may be blinded to perspectives and insights of men because their voice isn't represented in the PaC. This can be minimized by only moderating groups in which you're different from the members in an important way, such as a man running a woman-only group. You can also mitigate this by having a meeting guest or expert in the area in which there's an absence of perspective.
- These PaCs often have blind spots you'll have to mitigate through guest speakers, strategic roundtable discussions, or guest leaders. For example, religious groups may expect other business owners to operate like they do ethically, or they might find that the ways in which vendors or clients make decisions is contrary to their religious values. This can cause misalignment in working together.

4. Family Firms

Members: Family Firms have such a unique dynamic that they deserve special attention here. Members would be individuals from privately held Family Firms in any industry. The criteria are that the company is majority owned by a family and that this family is in primary control of the strategy and leadership.

Decision points:

- Do you have experience or knowledge of Family Firms' intricacies, challenges with succession, etc.? You must love and understand this type, or it could be frustrating to focus your PaC on it.
- Are there enough Family Firms geographically close to begin a local, in-person council, or will you have to be virtual?

Advantages:

- Their personal and business intersects are unique to family dynamics. There will be endless opportunities for help from their peers, and their peers will have plenty of stories and perspectives on both the personal and business levels.
- They find relief in discovering they're not alone in their family challenges.
- To participate in an environment of confidentiality is a breath of fresh air for them. Typically they're very private and don't discuss their business with anyone outside the family circle. Building trust takes time with their advisors like accountants, lawyers, bankers.

Disadvantages:

- Family Firms have business and personal challenges that other firms don't have. Since there's a tendency to be very private, there may be a reluctance to be vulnerable in a meeting. Vulnerability is vital for the best insights and issues to arise and be discussed deeply.
- There can be an initial reluctance to get involved in a PaC, as it could feel like airing dirty laundry.
- It can be frustrating to make decisions that appear to pit what's right for the business against what's right for the family. The result is often either indecision or Band-Aids, neither of which address the root problems.
- They have trouble deciding who should participate, particularly if there are cloudy boundaries and roles.
- They have difficulty getting all family members on board (which makes group decision-making challenging) and choosing one person to air or share challenges and opportunities with "strangers." (Do know that once they get past this, they enjoy engaging with other families, and work in this category can be very rewarding!)
- Getting the family to choose one member to participate and represent them can be difficult. The key is to work with the entire family first to get them comfortable with the concept, the benefits to them, and how they will all be supported by the individual participating as well as the entire group's participation.

TWO EXCITING TRENDS

The pandemic created a need for better collaboration methods. Plus, there's been a shift in business, emphasizing the more human aspects like advisory services and highlighting the importance of meaningful relationships as ways to retain and acquire new clients. The peer advisory industry can be the mechanism to accomplish those goals, as its value comes from human relationships. This is a whole new way of thinking for many, and it has resulted in PaCs that focus on customers as well as PaCs that are composed of people from within a company.

1. Client/Community

Any organization that has a large community of customers that it regularly interacts with has the opportunity to improve those relationships and expand their reach exponentially through PaCs. *How?* By creating and moderating PaCs composed entirely of their customers. Here's how it can work.

Accounting firms have a problem. They need to increase their advisory services (read: higher margin) to compensate for the commoditization of traditional services that now have lower margins. To make matters worse, new competitors are emerging offering these traditional services at no cost to lure clients to their firms. Additionally, partners are retiring, and transferring relationships to newer partners can be tricky. Finally, they want to retain their best clients and grow simultaneously. All of that is quite a tall order! And securing new clients is costly and time consuming, as it takes a lot of effort to build trust and relationships that will at some point translate into revenue.

How do accounting firms get to know their existing clients better—and strategically—while developing stronger bonds that allow them to serve the clients in a more personalized and proactive way? You guessed it—through a peer advisory council. Once again, think of the PaC as a mechanism to accomplish a firm's strategic initiatives. It can enable the accounting firm to build deeper relationships, offer a unique service to their clients, increase advisory services, and gain new clients.

> **Think of the PaC as a mechanism to accomplish a firm's strategic initiatives.**

The firm can participate as an advisor in the PaC or take a more arms-length approach and host the meetings and interact with the members for a bit prior to the start of the meeting. They can also pop in to showcase their expertise by sharing knowledge at strategic times throughout the year. Learnings from the meeting will be summarized by the moderator to protect confidentiality. They can then be shared with the firm to help the firm address common client challenges and opportunities. And last, if prospects are included, it's a no-brainer that eventually they would become clients because they're surrounded by other clients of the firm and get to regularly interact with the firm, if just for a few minutes.

2. In-Company

A company with a complex organizational structure is ideal for an internal PaC. Similar to the Community of Practice, this category of PaC consists of the company's employees—hence, *in-company*. But unlike the Community of Practice, this PaC has an intentional design and structure; it doesn't come together spontaneously or casually. The levels and types of interactions increase collaboration and improve problem-solving. Any topic or complex challenge that can benefit from different perspectives and insights can use a PaC as a way to surface those important thoughts. I'll discuss more about the actual methods used to bring out vital information during later chapters. For now, know that just deciding to organize an in-company PaC isn't enough, as there are pitfalls to look out for and better practices to follow to increase the chances of success.

• • •

Although any of these structures can make for a successful PaC, please know that you can also combine them if one doesn't sufficiently address the complexity of your idea. Combinations I've seen at my academy include the following:

- CEO (Position/Role) + Family Firms (Specialty)
- Woman Only (Specialty) + Local (Geography)
- Technology (Industry) + Global (Geography)
- COO (Position) + Private Equity (Client/Community)

Finally, there are always the mavericks. Every day, graduates from my training academy have created new niches to explore, like Kit Lisle, a Licensed Partner who's passionate about private equity companies.

Kit was a partner in a research-based consulting firm for private equity (PE) groups, family offices, and other private investors focused on relatively obscure niche subsegments. But a private equity company group as a whole is far too general, and Kit knows that. He decided to focus specifically on heads of operations within the PE firms. Why? Because leaders of operations have common challenges, and they're not in competition with each other like other leaders in a PE firm would be. For example, business-development leaders are pitted against each other. But operations leaders have a common goal—getting the best return on investment from their acquisitions of similar companies. They'll discuss how to leverage systems, how to integrate cultures and people, and how to not lose clients or talent. Talk about a niche! I hope it gets you thinking.

But Wait; There's More ...

When it comes to business PaCs, the amount of practice or experience a person has becomes important, as you need to match people according to their level of sophistication. There's no such thing as a one-size-fits-all council. I find it helpful to think about three levels of experience or sophistication, and your niche might have even more, though it's also possible that your niche might be complete and launchable without a discussion of levels.

> **There's no such thing as a one-size-fits-all council.**

1. **Entrepreneurial.** This level usually consists of new organizations and leaders or even serial entrepreneurs. I also include solo

entrepreneurs or those who are running a business more for lifestyle than legacy. Common characteristics: The companies are still developing their internal structure or the proofs of concept of their products or service offerings, and they have heavy foci on growing revenue and building processes. Their time is spent primarily (75 percent or more) on tactical, day-to-day activities, so they don't have much time for their strategic thinking.

2. **Growth.** This level usually consists of more established companies and leaders who are past the entrepreneurial phase. They have a solid business model and now are concentrating on scaling and growth. They're often concerned with expansion in their industry, gaining market share, or diversifying. The company typically has a strong foundation, structure, and client offerings, and the leaders are both tactical and strategic at a ratio of fifty-fifty.

3. **Strategic.** This level usually consists of seasoned, mature leaders who think strategically. The business is mature in many ways or large enough to have progressed to more complex, sophisticated, higher-level business practices. It's not uncommon to find both mature lines of business as well as new lines of business within the company. And the ratio is now 25 percent tactical to 75 percent strategic—the opposite of entrepreneurial.

As a professional trying to determine the right peer advisory council for you, these levels will assist you in determining the degree of sophistication you want in your members.

To Zoom or Not to Zoom

No discussion about creating a PaC is complete without a discussion about the legitimate concerns regarding virtual meetings. Prior to the COVID-19 pandemic, there were plenty of professional development, training, and Mastermind groups that were held virtually. But PaCs usually were primarily in person for several reasons:

1. Zoom, Microsoft Teams, and Google Meets simply weren't as prevalent; they weren't on the radar of many business owners. This can have a generational angle to it, as there are several generations who didn't grow up with virtual-meeting platforms or work in companies that used them. In other words, it's not something everyone had been exposed to prior to 2020.

2. Peer advisory council meetings aren't like the one-hour-ish Masterminds you probably get invited to weekly. They're hours long and involve deep discussion and reflection. Breaks might need to be frequent, and meetings might need to be shorter when you're virtual. If held in person, meetings are typically four hours, so maybe three is better or two two-hour meetings. The majority of business-PaC members aren't likely to choose virtual as a first choice unless they're comfortable with that amount of time in front of the camera. Furthermore, part of what makes a meeting in person special is the opportunity for sidebar conversations, the confidential environment, and the change of scenery from the office. For some, the commute to the meeting is even a plus, as they use it to prepare mentally for the meeting, and it becomes a ritual they enjoy.

3. When you're in person, you literally feel the other humans in the room. You feel their nervous systems and sense what's going on with them. This is because we're social mammals, and we have evolved for connection. The way you sit, the gestures you make, the energy your body seems to have … all of that is far easier to sense when you're in the room with someone. Meanwhile, virtual meetings typically only

allow you to see others from the chest or neck up versus the whole body. And with the advent of virtual backgrounds, who knows where someone is calling in from!

4. Virtual-meeting platforms have a major built-in distraction. Because they're accessed via computer, it's far too tempting to check email, answer notifications, surf the web, or scroll social media. It's imperative to have guidelines dictating that cameras must be on and that only the Zoom tab should be open.

5. Confidentiality and trust have to be assumed when virtual. You can't see who else is in the room, and you don't know who else might be listening.

6. PaCs have been around for a long time, and virtual meetings haven't. As a result, there's a mindset that the only way to do a PaC is in person, and it's too risky to try virtual. Another old mindset says virtual can't be better because members can't bond, pay attention, or embody the necessary elements of culture that a high-functioning council strives for. But time and the pandemic showed that virtual meetings have a place.

Meanwhile, there are plenty of reasons virtual meetings are actually preferable.

> *I have led both in-person and virtual meetings and found virtual meetings can be just as effective for the member experience.*
>
> —MARK WESTON, WASHINGTON, DC, CERTIFIED MODERATOR

1. It delivers a surprise benefit of supporting mental health. Once COVID-19 hit, everyone realized they could do almost everything virtually, which was wonderful. And something more important happened in my councils: we went from meeting monthly to weekly to daily. *Why?* Because members

needed support. They were extremely shaky due to the uncertainty the pandemic highlighted. They weren't certain that their biggest assets—their businesses—would survive. So many unknowns, so many moving parts rapidly changing. I had no idea how important meetings would become for the mental health of my members or how critical meetings would be for the health of their businesses. Their PaCs became safe spaces for them to be vulnerable, to talk through the enormous amount of information coming at them with the paycheck protection program (PPP) and restrictions, and to check their thinking on the vast number of quick decisions they were all having to make. They had already developed trust, and it was extraordinary to watch them lean on each other and look forward to their daily calls, even just to check in. As a result, the business grew 27 percent in the following few months! We were able to pivot into the virtual world and meet our clients' needs.

2. People who live in and near high-traffic, congested cities love virtual because they get burned out going back and forth in traffic or see it as a waste of time. Arriving on time to meetings has become unpredictable and frustrating to navigate, and we found that members love the option of virtual meetings interspersed with in-person meetings (more on this hybrid model in a bit).

3. Moderators who want the flexibility of not being tied to one specific location for monthly meetings find virtual a convenient, easy option.

4. Someone has tested positive for COVID-19, is recovering from surgery, or is caring for a family member. They don't

want to infect others, or they aren't mobile, and they can still participate fully and not have to miss their meetings.

5. Business owners who are also busy moms or dads on tight schedules or who have little ones at home without sitters or day cares love the virtual option. Single-parent business owners, for a variety of reasons, also benefit from virtual meetings.

6. Executives who travel a lot, whether temporarily or consistently, appreciate the flexibility of virtual. Virtual opens up the opportunity for them to participate in a PaC that's in person and has attendance expectations. For example, a member working on an acquisition that requires them to travel for a few months would miss in-person meetings, and you might lose them as a member or even a prospect because of that. But they could attend the in-person meeting virtually from a different location.

7. One of our Licensed Partners had this happen recently with a member doing an acquisition in a different country. He participated successfully for six months with his group virtually with new technology called the Owl. The Owl allows those attending remotely to view the room in 360 degrees, and the eye of the Owl moves to focus on whomever is talking. It mimics what you would see if you were there and is a win-win for everyone. For the Licensed Partner, this meant no turnover for the PaC, a retained member, and consistent participation from the engaged member, which benefited all the members. Finally, there were no reentry challenges when the member returned to the group six months later.

8. The cadence of the meetings is less likely to get disrupted when they're virtual. So if there's a snowstorm coming and

the meetings are in person, some or all members might not attend for fear of getting stranded. If the meetings were virtual, this would be less of an issue. Similarly, if the moderator gets stranded or is unable to get to an in-person meeting, a virtual meeting takes no time to set up.

Although a whole new world of acceptance opened up for virtual meetings because of COVID-19, and they are clearly beneficial and preferable in many circumstances, several years of virtual-only meetings has had some negative side effects, such as Zoom fatigue. Zoom fatigue has been called "a perplexing sense of being drained while having accomplished nothing" and can be decreased by turning off the camera; however, the camera provides necessary information and feedback, and turning it off isn't optional in many cases.[1] There can also be generational differences, with older people less thrilled by the idea of spending a lot of time online. If you were remote prior to COVID-19—and the majority of the workforce was *not*—it wasn't nearly as disruptive as getting dressed, driving to the office, and being in person with your team for years (or decades!), and then one day … not. For two years.

Furthermore, if you've ever been in the franchise business, you know that some franchises wouldn't allow virtual meetings because it implied that you might violate your territory restrictions. But again, once COVID-19 hit, just like for the rest of the world, adaptation to virtual became necessary.

Now that things have lightened up for many, lessons (and preferences) learned during the pandemic have revealed another way of delivering meetings—*the hybrid model*. As alluded to above, this is

---

1   Julia Sklar, "'Zoom Fatigue' Is Taxing the Brain. Here's Why That Happens," nationalgeographic. com (National Geographic, May 4, 2021), https://www.nationalgeographic.com/science/article/ coronavirus-zoom-fatigue-is-taxing-the-brain-here-is-why-that-happens.

a combination of in-person and virtual and can either be an actual, scheduled alternating of in-person and virtual meetings, or all meetings (assuming we're not all required to be remote again) are in person, and with the help of technology, members who can't make it in person that month can also participate.

Which Delivery Model Is Right for You?

You might not be a fan of virtual. Not before the pandemic, not during, and not now. And that's just fine! If you have to drag yourself on screen and muster up all of your energy to moderate an online meeting, and then you're exhausted thereafter, by all means, don't have virtual meetings.

At the same time, if you've chosen a global association of climate engineers for your PaC, you might want to rethink whether virtual isn't for you. In other words, your decision process could involve several factors and be a bit complex. Not complicated, but complex, and in need of contemplation of your options and what they mean for you as a moderator as well as your PaC members. Thinking long term about your lifestyle and business evolution is important as well because when you put your councils together correctly, they will last for years to come.

🧠 Takeaways

- Know your PaC so that you understand what constitutes conflict of interest between members.
- A combination of types of PaCs can create the perfect niche PaC for you.

- Virtual PaCs are acceptable methods of delivery, are effective for the right-fit members, and open up myriad opportunities for different types of PaCs.

🖾 Resources

- Scan the QR code at the back of the book to find a checklist for determining your right-fit PaC.

Now let's assemble your first PaC! Once you've decided exactly what kind of a PaC you want to moderate, it's time to choose your members one by one and always with an eye to what's best for the whole group.

CHAPTER 3

A Step-by-Step Guide to Assembling a Successful PaC

━━━━━━

Now that I've walked you through my process for identifying a peer group category and delivery model, we come to what might be the most overlooked area: assembling the group. Putting a group together is much more time-consuming and full of nuance than people new to the industry imagine. I'd love to say that the hardest work is choosing the most appropriate category for you and deciding whether the group will meet in person, but I'd be doing you a disservice if I didn't talk about the critical junctures of assembling a group. Here's what can happen when you don't put the proper attention and intention into choosing group members.

> Susan loved working with owners of privately held businesses. It didn't matter if they were founders of their companies, inherited their role in the family business, or took over for the owner when they retired. So it seemed logical that she would assemble a group

of presidents (position or role) in her city (geography) to meet in person (method) on a monthly basis.

Susan started by contacting her past clients and new clients to assemble her founding group. That was easy; she knew them and knew they would be a good fit together. This yielded her first three members. Then she announced on LinkedIn that she was putting a peer group together and reached out to CEOs she was connected to but didn't really know. Sound familiar? How many times have you accepted a connection from someone you didn't know? You just did it because, well, why not? And how do you think it went? Well, Susan was thrilled. She got some replies and invited those interested to the first meeting along with her known first three members.

Susan was so excited, as the LinkedIn connections seemed like they were slam dunks to be members. They were a bit skeptical, but she thought a meeting would convince them. How lucky she thought she was—they weren't a hard sell at all!

And this is where it went all wrong.

After the first meeting, Susan realized they weren't fitting in with the client members that she knew. In fact, it was a disaster. They weren't as experienced, and one was on the verge of bankruptcy and thought participating would save their company. Further-more, their personalities and values weren't aligned. Susan realized that when one of the new members talked about withholding payroll taxes to save money to expand a product line, she could see the shock and raised eyebrows on the faces of her members who were her past clients. And she couldn't get the other new member to stop boasting about their successes. It was like they were there to network, not to work on their business.

How could this happen, and what does Susan do now? How can she save the three members who were a right fit? Surely they would understand and let her fix this since she had worked with them in the past.

Scenarios like this aren't uncommon. Everyone who puts their first PaC together is almost 100 percent guaranteed to make mistakes, but most of them can be prevented. I've created a six-step, end-to-end process for putting groups together so they're high functioning and cohesive and stay together long term. I've taught this process to hundreds of PaC moderators, and it consistently produces groups that stretch each other's thinking, bond together, and grow together.

Six Steps to Assembling PaCs

1. Create a detailed profile of your ideal prospect.
2. Build partnerships to find your members.
3. Design a process for reaching out to them.
4. Make certain you're putting true peers together.
5. Assemble for diversity.
6. Confirm they will adhere to yours and the group's guidelines.

Let's take a dive into each one.

Step 1: Create a Detailed Profile of Your Ideal Prospect

Create this detailed profile, being aware that there might be more than one. Maybe there are a few types of people who would be a good fit together. With the list below, determine what characteristics you would enjoy and excel at working with and would be a good mix in the same group. The other angle is: What are the characteristics that describe a typical person in your chosen category? Once you settle on the details for each part, you'll put them together to get your ideal profile.

- **Knowledge level.** How much knowledge do they have about what they do? About their profession, about their role? Are they new to their role, or have they been in it for a while? Do they have a lot to share, or will they be soaking up all the information they can get?

- **Experience level.** How experienced are they at what they do? How long have they been doing it? Age isn't indicative of experience or knowledge. Some will have a wealth of experience in a short period of time, while others haven't grown much since they reached a certain level of expertise—they've plateaued.

- **Sophistication level.** How sophisticated is their business, and what level of maturity is it? Some businesses are complex, so their strategies are as well. Other businesses are more straightforward. All businesses will roughly fall into start-up stage, growth, or maturity. With each stage come advances in processes, people management, and overall techniques in running the business. A simple example using financials is this: a start-up will be learning the importance of doing financials with a solid P&L and balance sheet, and they'll probably outsource the work to an accounting firm or bookkeeper. A growth firm will typically have in-house accounting and maybe a controller and will have added a cash flow statement and some budgeting or KPIs to the mix. A more mature business will have all the above, and maybe a CFO, metrics, and timely reporting with strategic analysis. Which stage or stages of business do you want to work with?

- **Member location.** If the meeting is in person, is it realistically within driving distance? Take into consideration details in cities with bridges or perceived barriers that make it seem like it's too far to drive. For example, in Tampa Bay, Florida, people don't like to have to drive over the Howard Frankland Bridge between Saint Petersburg and Tampa; they prefer to stay on their side of the bridge for meetings. Or in Roanoke, Virginia, driving over the mountain to Blacksburg is perceived as being too far, even though it might not be that long of a drive. Where do you want to have the meetings? Does it matter to you? To your potential members?

In addition, you can also select for *the type of person* you want in your group. It just so happens that members in high-functioning, cohesive groups tend to share certain qualities. Here are my must-haves. Some people are just born with them, others have cultivated them, and yet others realize they're important and have started cultivating them, but they're just not there yet:

- Have a give-and-take mentality
- Value integrity and confidentiality
- Challenge others in a positive, constructive way
- Are committed to self-improvement
- Are nonjudgmental—seek to understand
- Have the willingness to be vulnerable

- Have a passion for lifelong learning
- Can check their ego at the door
- Will advocate for themselves and for others when they see or hear something concerning or problematic
- Are ready to do work that might be uncomfortable or difficult and are willing to leave their comfort zones
- Are open to new ideas and perspectives
- Realize they don't have all the answers and don't know everything about business

And there is a variety of reasons why someone might want to join a PaC. After running dozens of groups over two decades, I find these are the most popular "Whys" for PaC members:

- They've been getting the same unsatisfactory results over and over.
- They want to interact with peers on a deep level.
- They feel lonely in their roles or positions.
- They need to take time out of their businesses to be more strategic and proactive.
- They are not reaching their vision or goals fast enough.
- They want to give back and help others with their business experience.
- They're looking for a safe place to have candid conversations.
- They want more peace of mind, which translates to more confidence in making decisions, less stress from not knowing their blind spots, and relationships with peers they can count on to be there for them.

Meanwhile, there are red-flag qualities as well as red-flag Whys, which reveal someone who isn't a good match or who might want to join your group for the wrong reasons. For example, they may exhibit one or more of the following qualities:

- They are too self-absorbed—not willing to give and only wanting to receive or take.
- They want to join primarily for networking and business-development reasons.
- They aren't willing to change, preferring to complain about things that need changing.
- They are a joiner but not a doer. They won't implement suggestions to solve problems or execute on any commitments made.
- They won't be honest, and they play things very close to the vest. This will be an issue because they'll withhold essential information from the group, usually because they're embarrassed or ashamed of a past mistake. The group doesn't get the benefit of the lesson they learned because their pride is in the way.
- They view your group as the answer to all their immediate problems that need fixing. In other words, it's great to hear that a prospect is excited to join your group, but when someone is too eager, that could be a red flag. If a prospect's business is in shambles, and they're looking to the group to be a quick fix, that's a problem. That will not happen here. The ship has sailed for that prospect, and your group won't be able to save it in time.

These red flags will surface in your Discovery Call, the interview you perform to discern whether someone will benefit from being a member and whether your current members will benefit from the new addition. All you have to do is listen.

Keep Away from These Prospects

There are four rules of thumb for immediate rejection of a prospect. That sentence might sound unreasonable, but as you'll see, there are legitimate reasons for not wasting time with individuals who have certain qualities.

1. **They're not nice.** Avoid anyone who is rude to you, arrogant, mad at the world, or just mean. You haven't done anything to deserve their wrath, and they won't change. They won't treat you or their peers well.

2. **They're broke.** Don't take on a member who can't pay you long term. There are short-term exceptions, like waiting for a large contract payment to arrive. But outside of that, don't get sucked into thinking they'll figure it out. If someone's profit margin is that tight, they'll always be at risk of being a short-term member and disruptive to the group. Additionally, if they haven't been able to be profitable over a long period of time, why is that? The group cannot fix them as quickly as they probably need to be fixed. The most difficult part of this situation is that they won't tell you the truth. So if you sense it's bad, it's probably really bad. You'll have to go on what you're seeing, hearing, and feeling, as they're not going to come out and say they're broke.

3. **They don't want to work on the business.** They're there to sell to an audience of your ideal-profile members; their prospect's ideal profile is the same as yours. Typically, that's because they're the owner and top salesperson in their company. Don't think you'll flip their mindset, and they'll suddenly see the benefits of sharing with peers. They want revenue, and the growth of their business is their priority.

4. **Everything is great; nothing is wrong.** These people don't elaborate on their businesses or their roles. Instead, they have short answers and indicate everything is OK. Don't take on a new member who doesn't acknowledge that there's room for improvement and are opportunities to learn. There will be someone at some point who wants to join, but you can't figure out why. Don't take on a new member unless you can identify and articulate what they'll give and get from the group.

No matter how prestigious someone might be or how much you need another member, don't succumb to these four types of prospects. If you do, you'll be falling on your sword in a short few months, confessing your mistake to your members and engaging in the painful task of unwinding.

If you think about it,
what you need to do is be selfless.

If your focus when choosing members is *selflessness*, with your purpose as aiming to do whatever is the right thing to do to make the *entire* group successful, you'll be fine. Think of coming from the mindset of abundance versus scarcity. You want the mindset of abundance. You know that saying about accepting anyone with a pulse? Well, that doesn't work here. When you're not selfless, you make bad decisions that usually cost you later. Usually bad decisions are around money or trying to save time, meaning you're making a decision based on your needs, not the needs of the group. Trust me; I remember having a wonderful group that could have used one more member, and because I made some assumptions versus checking them out personally, I accepted someone I knew had good intentions, but I also knew something wasn't right about the fit.

I went against everything I teach because I was in a rush. It was a referral from a long-standing member. They knew what the good characteristics of a member are because they themselves had been a member for years. Why would they refer someone who wouldn't be a good fit for their group? I assumed they qualified them. First mistake: Don't make assumptions. The member didn't qualify the referral. But the second mistake was mine—I didn't do a thorough job of qualifying them myself because I trusted my member and assumed they did. And the third mistake was on me too—I didn't pay attention to my gut. I sensed the referral wasn't open when I talked to them. I also sensed their personality wasn't a fit for the group. I figured, Why would my member refer a person they didn't get along with? But what I didn't know was that my member didn't know the prospect. Again, I made an assumption. Fourth mistake. It was my member's business partner who had referred them. My member had never met them.

So what happened? They were a good member in many ways but irritated the other members endlessly. It was a style mismatch. I had to acknowledge that the person wasn't a good fit for the group. It was all on me.

When you make one bad decision, it impacts the whole group, and you can't hide it. There's an exponential risk for bad decisions. Why? All your customers know each other and impact each other, so one bad mistake can't be hidden as a 1:1 error, with only you and the

> **When you make one bad decision, it impacts the whole group.**

person directly involved being impacted. All members of that group know and are impacted. This is what I call *transparency without boundaries*. When a member leaves, you have to manage that one member's exit, but then you also have to explain the Why and do damage control with the remaining members of the group. One bad experience is multiplied across all the members. Where's the impact?

> The number-one issue in this industry is the failure to launch.

- **Extra time.** You have to manage the bad member's exit as well as talk to all the members about it. You can't just speak with the one ill-fitting member and call it a day.
- **Messaging.** You have to deliver the message about what happened, why, and why it won't happen again and apologize to the remaining group members.
- **Mindset.** You have to manage the mindset of the remaining members. They might be thinking the value of the PaC is lower due to the bad member taking a valuable seat in their group. Their experience was downgraded, and you'll need to be sure no one is at risk of resigning.

Step 2: Build Strategic Partnerships

Build Strategic Partnerships with individuals and groups who can help you find your ideal prospects or who already work with or are otherwise in contact with them. The number-one issue in this industry is the failure to launch. *Why?* Because most people who want to launch PaCs are doing it the hard way. They haven't updated their thinking and don't know how to sell to their ideal profile member the way that members like to buy. They're prospecting to people with their ideal-client profile *one at a time*, which is no longer effective. Most professionals do research prior to buying, and when it comes to speaking with someone new, they look for being referred or having some kind of prior knowledge of you. How do I get to know you prior to talking to you? Either through connecting with you by way of LinkedIn, blogs, regular newsletters, speaking events, etc. This is how we discern how credible someone is, and this is how partnerships are born.

In the early '90s, I was in charge of the Agent Partner Channel in the telecom industry. My goal was to expand our internal sales channel to include a sales channel outside the company's employee base. How could we leverage more sales without adding the same expense? And how could we reach new prospects we would otherwise not reach because of the relationships they had with someone else? Through Strategic Partnerships (SPs). The endeavor was so successful that I was listed as one of the Top Most Influential (Leaders) in Telecom.

I brought the idea of Strategic Partnerships into the peer group industry to help others launch successfully by leveraging the credibility of someone who already had their ideal client profile. This strategy provides instant credibility, gravitas, and access to the right-fit client. No more spending money solely on marketing tactics or lists, and no more time wasted attending networking events. For example, if your ideal client is the traditional midmarket CEO, then what organization already has them as clients? Accounting firms, commercial banks, payroll companies, wealth management, etc. Get creative, and you can find the right partner. Find out what organizations or vendors regularly work with your ideal clients. When you know those answers, you find your ideal SPs.

How does it work, and what's in it for the SP? The SP could be in the group as a member, but their role is usually that of a sponsor, in which they showcase their expertise through a brief presentation on a topic relevant to the group prior to the start of the meeting, and they leave before the meeting starts. The SP hosts the meetings in their location as well, but their main role is to involve *their* clients and prospects in *your* group(s). You're solving problems—*their* problems. Problems such as closing new clients, retaining clients, growing advisory services, and creating deeper relationships to be more proactive.

There are four key benefits for Strategic Partners:

1. You're helping them with business development by giving them the opportunity to establish new client relationships because they will invite their prospects to the group in addition to their current clients. And new clients equal more revenue.

2. Your group helps them identify their at-risk clients and add value, thereby increasing retention for them.

3. The profitability of their existing clients increases. Clients begin making better decisions and growing their businesses, and as they do, they need more services or more of the services your SP has.

4. They're positioned to have strategic conversations with their clients that increase client satisfaction, referrals, and retention. Having knowledge of strategy, vision, and challenges builds trust and leads to advisory conversations. These conversations build on the services or products the SP can provide that help the member achieve their goals.

You can have more than one SP for your PaCs. The key is to be sure they are complementary rather than in conflict with each other. By doing that, the value to the SP goes up because they now get access to someone else's clients or prospects who are also theirs.

The SP doesn't sit in the group unless they are also a member. Those two roles—SP and member—are different. The SP hosts the meeting and leaves the meeting before it starts. Their monthly time with the members is before the meeting starts in person or virtually or when you have a retreat or social with the group. Those are their opportunities for meaningful conversations. If the SP is also a member, they have to be willing to be vulnerable with their clients and prospects in the room as well as act fully like a member. I've seen this work very well with a bank CEO in the Midwest. Because of the CEO's vulnerability, the member felt so much respect for him and admiration for what he was trying to accomplish that they became clients of his if they weren't already!

The SP concept is a game changer that allows you to launch groups quickly and effectively and with minimal costs. It's a formal relationship where they agree to assist you in the introduction to their clients. Remember, they have an incentive to do so. So what's in it for you to have a SP? They're critical to your success because:

- They aid in your **business development**. This is a relationship business. Cold-calling isn't necessary or ideal. Being referred is ideal. That's why the SP concept is central to your success. Your leads will come from their introductions.
- The market recognition **enhances your brand** and credibility. Aligning with a reputable organization or person will enhance your brand and open doors to new opportunities.
- They help you identify **right-fit, ideal-client prospects**. Because you share the same profile, they've already vetted suspects to be prospects for you, which saves you a lot of

time qualifying them. By design, their clients and prospects should be qualified prospects for you.

- **They are a resource** for your members. You have an instant, ongoing, go-to resource that your members wouldn't have regular access to without you. Even if the member is a client of the SP, they don't interact regularly. You're providing content through your relationship with the SP that adds value to the membership and helps your members learn.

- **You're modeling** the advisor relationship for your members—showing them what it looks like. They remove skepticism that might exist about working with your SP's industry. We find this often with the banking, accounting, and law industries. Business owners traditionally want to keep them at arm's length out of fear, lack of trust, or the perception of being charged exorbitant rates for a quick question.

- **They (can) provide a venue for the meeting** that's professional, quiet, and neutral. This eliminates the confusion and uncertainty that arises when meeting venues change. You can control the professionalism of the environment and consistency of the meeting place. The better practice is to have a space that looks and feels like a boardroom and supports confidentiality.

- Strategic Partners provide **additional income streams**. Consider charging a fee for being your exclusive SP from each industry. Why a fee? *Why not?* A fee keeps the relationship top of mind but doesn't tilt it toward a mentality of "What have you done for me lately?" because the benefits to them are so integral to achieving their goals.

Step 3: Design a Process for Reaching Out to the Prospect

Design a process that takes into account their communication preferences. Do they like to be called, texted, emailed, messaged on LinkedIn? Is an introduction by someone else best? Remember the French Laundry experience? Every point of contact should be crafted to be appealing and convenient to the prospect. You want their first experience with you to be so good that they can't wait to sign up for more!

Here's a sample process that we teach in our academy and that will be a differentiator for you. Work with your SP or SPs to host a "sample meeting" or "test drive." Together, determine who should be invited. Ideally, all their clients and prospects should be on the list, but there could be exceptions. You might want to hold multiple meetings at different times and dates to accommodate vacations, holidays, or other commitments and to provide invitees options for attendance based on their preferences and availability.

The "sample meeting" is a standard approach to showing a prospect the value of participating in a PaC. It is a test-drive of a real meeting for the prospect's benefit. You physically set it up like a real meeting and have a sample agenda you'll follow. You'll do introductions and process someone's challenge, opportunity, problem, or idea (COPI—more about this in chapter 5). You'll close the sample meeting with details on your process of matching members, next steps, and takeaways, just like an actual meeting.

> **Prospects shouldn't sit in on existing meetings.**

You might be wondering why prospects shouldn't sit in on existing meetings in their entirety. Here's why that's not recommended: it degrades the confidentiality of the existing members, reduces vulnerability because of an unknown nonmember who hasn't committed yet, and isn't fair to those members who have committed and paid for their membership. Simply put, it's too risky. This is what could happen …

> I knew John, the potential member, fairly well and had in mind the right PaC for him. But he insisted on sitting in on a meeting as his way of being introduced to the process and the members. No matter what I said, he insisted. So I thought, "How risky can it really be to let him sit in on a real meeting? I mean, I do know him."
>
> He attended, and it was a disaster. He was not the guy I knew. He acted arrogant, was annoying and rude, and didn't listen. It was so bad that during a break, I told John he had to leave. I could see it wasn't a right fit. And then after the break, guess what I had to do next? Apologize to my existing members. (Remember the exponential impact one member has on other members? This is it!)
>
> Learn from me. No matter how much you talk yourself into believing it'll be fine, trust me when I say it won't. Hold sample meetings frequently throughout the year to allow your prospects to get a feel for the experience, and you'll always have a funnel of right-fit members to fill your group(s).

Other successful tactics that counter "I want to sit in on a meeting before deciding to be a member" are as follows:

- Offer a first-meeting guarantee. They must become a member, but if they aren't satisfied with their first meeting, you'll refund their first meeting dues. I've never had anyone ask for their money back. If you've qualified them properly as a good fit, they'll be a good fit, both from their point of view and the point of view of the other members.

- Have them meet another member or members one on one over coffee, lunch, or the phone. This is a good way for you to involve your members in the ownership of referring and vetting prospective members.
- Come to your meeting before it starts or after it closes to meet the members and interact with them. If it's in person, this can work extremely well if you're serving lunch before or after the meeting. They can then share a sandwich and get to know each other.
- Or ask the members for permission and have a member attend a specific part of the meeting like the opening, or the processing of their COPI, or the SP presentation part, to get more of the experience.

Here are some other popular ways to find right-fit members:

- **Centers of Influence.** Colleagues that can help refer or connect you to possible prospects. They want to help you and genuinely want you to succeed. So anything they can do to assist they will.
- **LinkedIn.** Making connections and using the search function will uncover potential prospects for you. Reach out to them via an InMail, or ask for a connection you share to make an introduction. Many times those launching groups use this as the main source of leads as well as mailing lists. Rare is it that someone is able to get a group launched with this method alone. I witness time and time again that they have

to hire outside LinkedIn experts to help connect with their ideal profile. And while it can work, with the right firm, it's expensive and not guaranteed.

- **Networking organizations.** You can join these organizations solely for the purpose of business development. The more exclusive they are, the more expensive it is to be a member. Be sure before joining, however, that the members have the connections matching your ideal member profile.

These three methods can supplement your SP alliance. I'm always a fan of having a plan B, as more options are always preferable to no options. There are plenty of unknowns and things you have no control over, and backup plans can be business and time-savers!

Step 4: Make Certain You're Putting True Peers Together

And "true peers" doesn't mean twelve people who are practically clones of each other. True peers are the secret sauce to long-term retention, a high-functioning group, referrals, and pure joy for you as a moderator.

How do you ensure that someone is a true peer? Through the next, and extremely crucial, step after the sample meeting: the Discovery Call.

The Discovery Call is an interview that can be done in person or over the phone—Zoom or no Zoom. I've perfected the ability to discern and close a right-fit member over

Think of yourself more like a recruiter.

the phone, but if you believe the best method for you is in person, do it that way, particularly if you're building a group locally. Either one can work. Whichever way you go depends on your preference and sometimes the preference of the prospect.

Notice I used the word *interview* earlier. You aren't "selling" anyone. No one wants to be sold to anymore, unless they're a salesperson, in which case they love it! I know because I'm a true salesperson at heart, and I have been certified in about every sales method there is. You do not need those methods to be successful here. Think of yourself more like a recruiter. You're recruiting for your PaC, and success is matching the candidate (the prospect) with the company (your PaC) and vice versa.

The Discovery Call method I use has three parts:

1. Find out how they got to where they are. Go back to the beginning, from childhood to the present day. You're listening for the experiences they've had, where they are right now, where they want to go, and how they'll relate to participating in your council. For example, if you're looking for a business owner for your council, you'll be listening for their values, integrity, failures, learnings, successes, and opportunities and getting a sense of their overall genuine personality. Why? Because you're going to match those answers with the answers of your other prospects and members. More on that below.

2. Identify their FORD. **The FORD Method** is a research-backed technique to build relationships. It's an excellent way to build rapport with people by asking them a series of questions and listening closely to their answers, which drive your further questions.

When you ask people about their family, occupation, hobbies, and goals, you find out what they truly value as well as what they're looking to achieve in life. Plus, those conversations build trust by demonstrating your investment in the person beyond the initial transaction. You'll become a Resource Connector (more on that in chapter 4)!

Family. Since most people have a family they tend to talk about, this topic makes for an easy icebreaker. Remember that the concept of family isn't just about blood relatives. Many people also consider their business partners, friends, or pets as part of their family. You can build on what they share with you to ask more thought-provoking questions.

Sample questions: *Tell me about your childhood; where did you grow up? What was your favorite part? Who in your family had the most influence on you? How did the two of you meet (if you're meeting a couple for the first time or they mention they are married)? How old is your child (children)?*

Occupation. One of the easiest topics to start a conversation with is what someone does for a living. It's where they spend most of their waking hours. Most people have some form of occupation, although in some cases, work is the last thing they want to talk about. People's jobs or educations are often related to something they're passionate about, so this information can provide insight into their interests.

Sample questions: *Describe how you got to where you are today. How did you get involved in that line of work? What's your favorite part of your role? What skill do you excel in? What's the highest and best use of your time?*

Recreation. This refers to anything people do for relaxation or enjoyment. It's all about having fun! You can easily get to know someone on a more personal level by finding out what they like to do in their spare time.

Sample questions: *What's your favorite thing to do for fun? What's the most interesting thing you've done or an interesting place you've visited? Do you go on holiday often? If so, when did you go most recently, and where to? What do you do to relax or get reenergized?*

Dreams. Aspirations and goals help us reach for more in life. Dreams can reveal a lot about a person's inner world. They might also open the door for deeper conversations. Asking about dreams is fun, and asking open-ended questions will make things flow easily. While talking about dreams may not always be appropriate for initial small talk, dreams can become beneficial when you've already established a connection with someone and want to probe more deeply.

Sample questions: *What's your vision for your business? What do you want your role to look like in the future? What's on your bucket list? What's a big dream you have?*

At the end of this chapter, I've included a FORD worksheet so you can see how I use it with prospects.

3. **The Four-to-One Ratio:** A technique to help you have an in-depth, meaningful conversation is what I call the four-to-one ratio. For every answer given to your question, ask three more questions off that answer. For example:

Question 1: *Where did you grow up?*

Answer: I grew up in Missouri on a farm.

Question 2: *Really? What kind of farm was it?*

Answer: It was a one-thousand-acre farm where we had cattle and also harvested corn, soybeans, and wheat.

Question 3: *Wow, did you work on the farm when you grew up?*

Answer: Yes, I did. I drove the tractor, planted the crops, drove the trucks to the grain bins, fed the cattle, rounded up the cattle, and did all that farm stuff you hear about.

Question 4: *Do you miss that life?*

Answer: I do. It was a great environment to grow up in.

The instant vulnerability displayed by the person answering the question can be amazing while being predictable if the questioning is done skillfully. By answering a series of questions that build upon each other, what I call *narrow questioning,* a feeling of being heard is experienced. That feeling of being heard during the four-to-one allows for further openness, vulnerability, and honesty.

How is this achieved by the person asking questions? What exactly are they doing to elicit openness? They listen. Without good listening skills, the narrowing questioning won't seem genuine and authentic. In the end, both parties should have built a closer relationship of trust and knowledge—what we define as a meaningful conversation. And that only happens through supportive, generous listening. This puts you on the path to determining whether this person is a fit for your PaC.

A WORD ON DIVERSITY AND GOOD INTERVIEWING SKILLS

Once you know more about the human side of the prospects for your groups, it becomes easier to discern who among them are true peers. Again, this doesn't mean you want twelve people who are clones. It means you want twelve people who are similar in important ways, yet within the group, various perspectives are represented: genders, ethnic backgrounds, ages, and types of experience. Remember, if you have a group made up of the same type of people, you risk groupthink.

Having diverse perspectives well represented in your PaC is invaluable to the member experience.

We've received countless accolades from members who appreciate and value the diversity in their PaCs. They usually don't have diversity around them in their own teams and certainly don't trust biased feedback. Having diverse perspectives well represented in your PaC is invaluable to the member experience. It might seem contradictory, but what you want is

- diversity of experience and commonality of experience, and
- diversity of perspective and commonality of perspective.

In other words, your members should overlap in important ways, but they should also be different in important ways. So they share some aspects of experience in and with what they do—for example, a PaC of CEOs—but they also bring significant differences to the table, such as the fact that they work in different industries.

When novices attempt to assemble groups, a common mistake is putting CEOs and business owners together based on revenue and the number of employees. But that doesn't tell you what you need to know about their level of sophistication, experience, and knowledge. Those stats might be good to know, but they're not necessary for matching true peers. In fact, I've successfully matched members many times without ever knowing their numbers. I can tell by their answers where they are in size, complexity, experience, and sophistication. You don't need numbers to tell you that; you need great questions.

True peers are revealed through the interview process. You learn your prospect's past experiences, future desires, values, challenges, and type of business, as well as what they excel at, what they don't, how they think, how they solve problems, and what they've learned along the way, and then you match them with others according to synergies. You listen for how one member's challenge is another's expertise. One member's experience is another's future opportunity or strategy. Maybe there are similarities in structure or type of client. You want them to think differently from each other because that's how you create *aha* moments. It's like a big matrix. You're looking for areas in which there are complements and differences, making sure their sophistication levels and values match.

When you intentionally search for diverse, right-fit candidates, you'll find them. What you can't do is just hope that it happens or take the easy route of finding any company that can be a right fit but doesn't add diversity into the equation. While it makes adding a member to your group harder, in the long run, you're building a stronger PaC that will have many more benefits than a nondiverse group. You're operating at a higher level and creating a unique experience your members cannot replicate on their own. But more important, having a diverse group gives your members a variety of thoughts, approaches, perspectives, insights, and learnings that will give them better chances of reaching their goals.

Step 5: Assemble for Diversity, Equity, Inclusion, and Belonging

It needs to be said that diversity of perspective and experience doesn't necessarily equate to what is known as diversity, equity, inclusion, and belonging, or DEIB. I trust you've read some of the numerous articles written about corporate America's diversity problem and the benefits of having a diverse board of directors. For example, *Why*

Diversity Matters, an often-cited 2015 McKinsey & Company report, claims that diversity on corporate boards benefits the bottom line. In a study of 366 public companies in Canada, Latin America, the United States, and the United Kingdom, companies with boards that ranked in the top quartile for racial diversity were 33 percent more likely to outperform those in the bottom quartile. In addition, those in the top quartile for gender diversity were 21 percent more likely to outperform those in the bottom quartile. With that said, a less homogenous board doesn't necessarily guarantee higher profits, although the McKinsey report noted, "More diverse companies, we believe, are better able to win top talent and improve their customer orientation, employee satisfaction, and decision making, all that leads to a virtuous cycle of increasing returns."[2]

Articles and statistics about diversity have been so prevalent that new mandates and rules are being enforced by governments and the financial markets. It's both common sense and logical to understand that diverse boards, diverse leadership, and a diverse workforce all bring valuable insights, opinions, and perspectives to solving problems—different perspectives that can make a good decision a great decision. Wouldn't you rather have great decisions rather than mediocre decisions?

Most of what has been written addresses how public corporations benefit from diversity. But what is the benefit for privately held companies?

---

2   Vivian Hunt, Dennis Layton, and Sara Prince, "Why Diversity Matters," https://www.mckinsey.com/ (McKinsey & Company, January 2015), https://www.mckinsey.com/~/media/mckinsey/business%20functions/people%20and%20organizational%20performance/our%20insights/why%20diversity%20matters/why%20diversity%20matters.pdf.

DEIB and the PaC

Formulating an annual strategy plan for my PaC helped uncover some of my personal and council blind spots. Lack of diversity in our council was our most recent. As a result, we intentionally have closed the gap and are creating a better member experience.

—ROSS PASSANTINO, PASSANTINO MARKETING;
CERTIFIED MODERATOR, KANSAS CITY

A diverse peer advisory council can do much more than "check the box" or act as a feel-good.

Diversity in your PaCs will do the following:

- Expand the knowledge, experience, and insight that go into a member's decision-making because they have different experiences that shape their viewpoints.
- Create *aha* moments from looking at something from a different lens.
- Create clarity around why a particular problem keeps surfacing.
- Cover areas members need to attend to that they didn't know they had.
- Solidify and expand the culture of the member's business by showing the benefits of working with people with different backgrounds.
- Help educate them about the thinking of different genders and ethnic backgrounds.
- Expand their leadership skills beyond their comfort zone by working with peers who think differently.
- Give everyone in the group a true competitive edge in the marketplace because their minds will expand, they will become

more curious about the experiences of others, and they will gain actual experience with people very much unlike them.

When the Black Lives Matter movement emerged, many business leaders of privately held companies didn't think they needed to address their teams about what was happening. They thought the issue was more for the "big" corporations and not them. They believed that silence was fine and that there was no need to bring up the subject unless someone on the team did. They felt there wasn't a need to articulate the company stance and expectations for how others should be treated or a commitment to a more diverse workforce. They felt that if everything seemed fine, they shouldn't rock the boat with what they perceived would be a political statement. However, saying nothing is saying something—it speaks to what you believe and what you value. Silence isn't silence.

The peer groups with diverse members of race and gender thought otherwise. They communicated with their employees about the topic. They made a plan for filling the gaps in key positions with diverse team members and sought out applicants who were differently abled, not neurotypical, and gender nonconforming. Why? Because their fellow members explained the value in doing so. As a result, their teams had more open discussions, became more vulnerable because they felt safe, voiced their ideas about opportunities for diversity, and offered to help and lead initiatives. Overall, this strategy increased company engagement and employee retention as well as led to acquiring talent. They showed they understood a key issue in today's society, rather than either talking about it and doing nothing or not talking about it at all.

I'd be remiss if I didn't mention some of the challenges regarding diversity. For instance, if you're creating a diverse, in-person CEO peer group, the reality is that some geographies make that difficult. Some areas of the country have clusters of one race and not others.

For example, the District of Columbia has a higher number of Black CEOs running privately held businesses than Osage Beach, Missouri, per capita. That doesn't make either area good or bad; it's just a demographic fact. The pool of diverse business owners in some areas can be very small, as most business owners still today are white males. This makes forming a diverse group with true peers difficult, particularly in smaller, rural communities.

Relatedly, there are numerous minority businesses under $500,000 in revenue, but they're typically not good fits for the traditional CEO or senior leader PaC. They're not past infancy, don't tend to be strategic, and in some cases are intentionally solo entrepreneurs. This further reduces your pool of candidates.

Then there's the name challenge. It can be easy to identify some business owners' genders and races by their names but not always. This makes it tough to identify candidates you're looking for. Talking to the local chamber of commerce and other business organizations can help you with this. Especially speak with any diversity organizations in your area, such as the Urban League. A list can be found at https://ofm.wa.gov/state-human-resources/workforce-diversity-equity-and-inclusion.

The Special Case of Women-Only PaCs

Most people's intuition tells them that an all-female peer advisory council would be more beneficial for women than one that includes both men and women. But that's far from always the case; there are pros and cons to women-only PaCs.

Similarly, on the business front, I could see why it would be a good idea to have a women-only group of business leaders who are moms—particularly new moms. Balancing new motherhood with the pressures of running a business or otherwise working full time adds to the complexity of managing emotions, perceptions, and new challenges. Some of these challenges would be unique to women in this situation.

According to LeanIn and McKinsey & Company's *2020 Women in the Workplace* report:

> *The pandemic has intensified challenges that women already faced. Working mothers have always worked a "double shift"—a full day of work, followed by hours spent caring for children and doing household labor. Now the supports that made this possible—including school and childcare—have been upended. And if a woman is a single parent, the "double shift" is monumental.*[3]

The report goes on to say:

> *Senior-level women are also nearly twice as likely as women overall to be "Onlys"—the only or one of the only women in the room at work. That comes with its own challenges: Women who are Onlys are more likely than women who work with other women to feel pressure to work more and to experience microaggressions, including needing to provide additional evidence of their competence."*[4]

Women business owners face greater challenges accessing capital, resources, and mentorship, in part because unconscious bias and institutionalized barriers stand in the way of such access.

For women in executive leadership as well women business owners, being part of a group of like-minded female leaders who can

---

3   "Women in the Workplace 2022," mckinsey.com (McKinsey & Company, October 18, 2022), https://www.mckinsey.com/featured-insights/diversity-and-inclusion/women-in-the-workplace.

4   Kevin Sneader and Lareina Yee, "One Is the Loneliest Number," mckinsey.com (McKinsey & Company, March 22, 2021), https://www.mckinsey.com/featured-insights/gender-equality/one-is-the-loneliest-number.

relate to those challenges may be beneficial to the growth of their careers and their businesses.

The argument to be made against women-only PaCs that don't specifically revolve around the idea of motherhood and its challenges, is, well, diversity. Being in a confidential environment with men can give women support, insight, and a different perspective. This is particularly true if their similarity—the core idea of the group—is their position. For instance, mom or not, if you're the CEO of a global company, you want as many perspectives in the room as possible to help you see what you don't see.

> **Varying perspectives can make the difference between a good decision and a great decision.**

I go into all of this in depth because part of your job is to carefully and intentionally select members for your group that represent different perspectives, and sometimes we don't see that we're closing the group off from important perspectives. Remember, varying perspectives can make the difference between a good decision and a great decision. They can make the difference between being a proactive leader and a reactive leader.

Step 6: Set Your PaC Expectations, and Confirm That Members Will Adhere to the Group's Guidelines

This starts with you listening in your interview (Discovery Call) for their ability to adhere to the guidelines you have for your PaC. What are guidelines? They're rules and expectations set and agreed to by the members regarding how the PaC will function. The following chapter will get into the guidelines and provide a sample.

For now, just know that if the group has established guidelines, each new member should be made aware of them and sign off on them before committing to membership. The sign-off could be a separate document or part of your membership application.

It's time to get into the details of designing your member's experience, moving toward providing the French Laundry levels of satisfaction and value.

💡 Takeaways

- FORD and four-to-one are narrow-questioning techniques to identify right-fit members.
- Use the knowledge, experience, and sophistication of a prospect over revenue and number of employees to determine fit.
- Listen for why a prospect would be a great member and also why they wouldn't.
- Your ability to launch will depend on the connections and partnerships you've developed.
- Discovery Calls are just as much about the prospect evaluating you as you evaluating them.
- Diversity is essential to providing the ultimate member experience.

📇 Resources

At the back of the book, you'll find a QR code that will direct you to these key resources:

- Ideal member profile sheet,
- FORD worksheet, and
- Sample Discovery Call questions.

CHAPTER 4

Designing the Initial Experience

━━━━

You may have heard the term "customer experience" (CX). For every CX, there's a designer of that experience. Whether the product is a service or an online course, the designer of the CX wants to create an experience for their customer that's of such high quality that they continue to use the service or rave about the course to anyone who will listen. They are loyal and vocal. And make no mistake: everyone from the designers of the product to the marketers of the product to the designer of the experience knows that we live in a time when trust, connection, and communication with customers are crucial to the success of a product's launch and sustainability. The customer has the advantage because they have more choices than ever, and

> **We live in a time when trust, connection, and communication with customers are crucial to the success of a product's launch and sustainability.**

they can *and will* take their business elsewhere, *and write a bad review,* if they're not satisfied.

You, the moderator, are essentially the designer of your members' experiences (MX). As such, your goal is to create an experience so memorable that the members of your peer advisory council can't find anything to compare it to. This is what we call the Disney Effect.

Have you ever been to Disneyland or Disney World? I actually haven't! My parents tried to take me when I was eleven years old. We never took family vacations while living on the farm, but one year we did. The highlight of that vacation for me was to visit Disney World. We drove to Florida, and that Monday morning, we got up early so we could beat the crowd and get into Disney World before anyone else. I vividly remember driving into the huge parking lot; I thought it was so big because there were no cars there. They must all be somewhere else. No. At 7:00 a.m. that Monday morning, my parents learned that Disney World was closed on Mondays! Yes, closed. You can imagine the disappointment of an eleven-year-old and the horrified looks on my parents' faces. We had an affinity for Walt Disney. He spent his boyhood years on a farm outside Marceline, Missouri, which was 26.7 miles from Triplett, the town I lived closest to. To this day, Disney World is on my bucket list.

Walt Disney believed the most critical element of the theme park experience was consistent, quality service. Constant repetition and mastery of small tasks led to an overall "magical" experience. No wonder first-time Disney visitors have a return rate of 70 percent! It's the land of happy, cheerful people, cleanliness, and consistency. Staff are helpful, willing, and delighted to spend time with you.

Your Disney euphoria typically lasts seventy-two hours. During the time after leaving the park, you compare every interaction to what you've just experienced. You look at everything through the Disney prism—Is it as clean? Are the people as helpful? Do they anticipate your every need?—and more. It's almost impossible for anyone to overcome the Disney Effect the initial seventy-two hours after they've been there. Nothing will seem as good. What if the PaC meetings you moderate leave the members similarly euphoric afterward? Wouldn't that be amazing?

The Disney Effect's Revenue Effect

If it seems like a lot of work attending to all of the details that would result in a Disney Effect, what if I told you that there's a return on that experience-creation investment? InfoQuest, a provider of internet hosting and data center services, analyzed customer satisfaction data from the findings of more than twenty thousand customer surveys conducted in forty countries. The conclusions of the study established a link between customer satisfaction and revenue:[5]

- A totally satisfied customer contributes 2.6 times as much revenue to a company as a somewhat satisfied customer. Translation for you: If your monthly dues are $1,000, a totally satisfied member will then contribute the equivalent of $2,600 a month. This will show up in how long they stay as a member or what we call the lifetime value of a client (LTV) and in additional services or referrals to you.

- A totally satisfied customer contributes 14 times as much revenue as a somewhat dissatisfied customer. Translation for you: Using the above example of $1,000 monthly member dues, if dissatisfied, they will terminate their membership and probably tell a few people about their less-than-satisfactory

---

5   "Survey Case Studies," https://www.infoquestcrm.co.uk/ (Info Quest CRM, June 16, 2020), https://www.infoquestcrm.co.uk/case-studies-2/.

experience. But a satisfied member will last $14,000 worth more than the $1,000 dissatisfied member.

Satisfied customers create lasting revenue for you.

How do you create the Disney Effect in your groups? Here are a few tips:

- Demonstrate a sense of humor in your agendas, reminder meeting emails, and follow-up conversations to make them memorable. For example, a moderator I knew would always include silly and funny trivia in their email reminders. Over time, people got used to this, and everyone eagerly awaited their arrival.

- Plan thoughtful agendas that relate to exactly what the group needs. For example, if everyone is focused on improving their digital marketing, you might buy a digital marketing book for each member and bookmark key points or host a webinar for the members with a digital marketing expert.

You may be familiar with a quote by Dell's Jerry Gregoire from over twenty years ago: "The customer experience is the next competitive battleground."[6] Well, that time has come, and differentiating yourself through a stellar MX is vital to your success.

BE A RESOURCE CONNECTOR

As a moderator, you're the conduit—the means to connect your members to each other or to others who can be of help to them. This will come naturally when you employ the FORD techniques

---

6   Scott Kirsner, "The Customer Experience," https://www.fastcompany.com/ (Fast Company, 1999), https://www.fastcompany.com/56447/customer-experience.

and four-to-one together. Listening to the answers will spark ideas about how you can be of help.

The members also look to you as the spoke of the wheel—the place where everything comes together and intersects in one place. You'll have insights that others won't have. Your goal is always to make the members look good to each other and connect to each other for answers rather than you being the only one with answers.

> **Being a Resource Connector deepens your relationship with the member. They know you've listened to them and have their best interests at heart.**

Being a Resource Connector deepens your relationship with the member. They know you've listened to them and have their best interests at heart. You show you care. The key is for them to feel like you care about their business as much as they do.

Be as committed to their success as they are.

Here are some examples of being a Resource Connector:

- A member asks you for help getting information about a business practice. You know the answer, but instead you refer them to someone in the group you know has the answer too.
- You know a member is getting ready to travel to Napa Valley. You recommend the top three or four restaurants for them to enjoy based on their favorite type of food. You might even connect them with the chef of one of the restaurants.

- One of the common recurring sidebar questions that members ask each other and you, is "Do you know a person?" which you may have heard as "Do you know a guy?" At some point, your member needs referrals to people. This includes business referrals, such as a payroll provider or an HR consultant, and personal referrals, such as a caterer for a party or a landscaper. You never know what you might be asked, but the key is *Do you know someone who knows someone?* so you can help your member save time and be connected to a resource quickly and reliably.

The ABCs of Sales

In the movie *Glengarry Glen Ross*, Blake (played by Alec Baldwin) addresses a room full of sales associates and shares what he believes is a fundamental lesson about sales. He calls the lesson "ABC," which stands for "Always Be Closing." This reflects the traditional view of sales: that achieving success in sales is all about drive, persuasion, and a commitment to be selling all the time.

Glengarry Glen Ross was published in 1983 and won the Pulitzer Prize in 1984. You know what didn't exist in 1984? The internet. Our world is now a vast network of networks, and with that advancement have come new and more effective ways of working, which includes revised best practices in sales. The moderator isn't just connecting with the group members; they're connecting the members with their network as well as with each other. This is all part of the experience you are creating with your members.

The OLD ABC in business

A = ALWAYS
B = BE
C = CLOSING

The NEW ABC in business

A = ALWAYS
B = BE
C = CONNECTING

Let's Create That Remarkable Experience!

In chapter 3, I introduced the ideal prospect profile and how Strategic Partners can help you find them. I mentioned the sample meeting as well as the importance of passing on people who aren't good fits.

The moment an ideal prospect says yes, you should send them their agreement to sign and schedule a date for their Orientation that's contingent on the existing members' approval. Orientation is a one-on-one meeting to prepare them for their first PaC meeting. In essence, you're training them and planning with them for that meeting. This can be done virtually; however, bonding is usually easier in person, and your priority at this moment is cultivating trust and connecting with them.

The Orientation should include delivering value immediately, thereby reinforcing their decision to join and reducing the likelihood of *buyer's remorse*. Delivering value is in the eyes of the beholder, but examples can be reviewing a leadership assessment they completed as part of Orientation or helping them gain clarity on the first COPI (again, that stands for Challenge, Opportunity, Problem, or Idea and is discussed in the next chapter) they will raise in the meeting. Orientation should also lay the foundation for what to expect and eliminate unknowns.

One of those expectations is that existing members of the PaC have the opportunity to decline a new member based on a conflict of interest. You've already vetted them, but maybe an existing member knows something you don't know. If there's any conflict of interest from an existing member, you want to know before the new person joins, as it's only a matter of time before that becomes a problem ... for everyone. It's most efficient to send existing members the basics—the name of the potential new member, company, and website—prior to their Orientation. Simply set the expectation with the words "New Member Approval" in the subject line, and it shouldn't take long. Send the information, even if there's just one new member. There's always your first member, and they get that courtesy too! If a member indicates there's a conflict, you need not say anything to the potential new member other than a conflict of interest has surfaced. In fact, for confidentiality reasons, you shouldn't ever elaborate as to who or what it is. Protecting your existing members is your priority. It doesn't matter what the conflict is or with whom; the fact is it's present, and that is all you need to know.

Sometimes you or your members will want to be more involved in the process of selecting the new member. This is a good thing that can also be a bad thing. Good, because it demonstrates that the members are taking ownership and making the group their own. Good, also because they care and want to help recruit right-fit members. Bad, because it can slow the process. Sometimes members have great intentions but not great follow-through because of their busy schedules. This can cause issues with scheduling and timeliness and result in bad first impressions for the new person. It can also be bad because you don't want to give members the ability to reject someone who would be ideal for the group. This usually shows up around diversity when the group rejects someone who is unlike them. Be on the lookout for homogeneous groups being closed to someone different. If you include members as part of the process, be sure to have agreed-upon expectations to eliminate this risk.

Once you have approval from existing members, you can proceed with the scheduled Orientation or schedule it if you haven't yet.

Orientation: When Does It Start?

All successful Orientations begin with thorough preparation. Thoroughness is based not on what you want to do, but on what you think the new member can digest, and that can be tricky. Pay attention to their patience level and bandwidth, and with the help of assessments such as DiSC and Predictive Index, you can determine what to provide them with and when.

In my mind, Orientation starts when you have the membership application back and approval from existing members. Prepare the member by sending calendar invites, the current member roster, member profiles if you have them, and a thank-you note for becoming a member. You might also send an agenda or questions for the member to answer and be ready to share. Some members will be detailed and very organized, which will be evident based on the timeliness of their replies. Some might not reply at all. This gives you a sense of whether you have a responsive member or a challenged or challenging, unresponsive member. It doesn't mean one will be a better member in the meeting than the other. What it means is that you haven't figured out the best communication method for the member who didn't immediately respond, you haven't set expectations, or you don't understand the style of that person.

> Set the bar high, and you'll get exceptional participation. Set the bar low, and you'll get bad behavior and poor participation.

First impressions set the stage for your new member. If you're lax, they'll be lax. If you're organized, that will give them the impression they can rely on you. If you've set expectations, they'll realize this is how you run your meeting, and they'll be expected to step up to adhere to those standards. Set the bar high, and you'll get exceptional participation. Set the bar low, and you'll get bad behavior and poor participation.

Next is setting the member at ease and beginning to build the bond with the other members. A new member will usually be anxious about what the other members are like. This is when impostor syndrome kicks in, and everyone worries they'll be found out—people will realize they're not as successful or as good a leader as people think they are. They also wonder what everyone wears to the meeting if it's in person, how prepared everyone will be, and whether they'll be accepted. They're basically the new kid arriving at school after the year has already begun, and they're anticipating a dreadful first day. But once you tell them all they have in common with their new classmates, their anxiety will be alleviated.

How do you cover all of this and give your new member a remarkable first experience with Orientation? Here's a basic outline we teach in our academy that has proven to be the right amount of information and setting of expectations for a new member to show up strong from the start and be wowed by your process and your PaC.

TEN-POINT NEW MEMBER ORIENTATION FORMAT

1. Welcome and objective of the meeting.
2. Review your and the group's expectations and guidelines.
3. Give overview of existing members' businesses.
4. Highlight what various members have in common with the new member.
5. Review results from their assessment (if any).
6. Explain the meeting structure and methodology behind it.
7. Review what you'd like them to include in their introduction to the group at the first meeting.
8. Plan what their first COPI will be to the group and when it will be delivered—in the first meeting or a subsequent meeting.
9. Record what they expect to gain from membership. What does a remarkable experience look like for them? This is a good time to review what the member can expect in their journey. We have a map outlining this at the end of the chapter as a resource.
10. Confirm that all meetings are on their calendar and they have your contact information saved.

You have to consider how much time you have in Orientation to know how much time to spend on each point. Ideally, you have an hour, and that's all you need. If this isn't a virtual group, face-to-face Orientation is usually better for bonding, and you can see their environment, which tells you a lot about them.

Guidelines for Peer Advisory Council Meetings

Guidelines are sets of expectations and processes that allow the meetings to run smoothly and the members to interact productively. They directly impact the experience of the members. The guidelines create the culture of the peer advisory council, and absent explicit guidelines, the group will naturally generate its own default culture, which may or may not work for you and the group. Peer advisory councils run best and are easier to moderate when there are guidelines. Meanwhile, a lack of intentional culture usually creates dysfunction that ultimately leads to member turnover. There are two types of guidelines: (1) for the behavior expected from group members (also called soft guidelines), and (2) for the specifics of how the group will run (hard guidelines). Soft and hard guidelines support each other and are both necessary for the PaC's short-term success and long-term sustainability.

Soft guidelines include the qualities that make a good member from chapter 3. An extension of them is a list of six attributes I've identified that contribute to a high-functioning group. They'll take time for your members to develop individually and then as a group. It's important to name them at least. Whether or not they end up spelled out in guidelines for your PaC depends on what you all decide together.

1. **They have respect for diversity of opinion and perspective.** Members don't expect everyone to believe or think like they do. They understand that different perspectives provide different insights that help them solve incredibly difficult problems. Diversity also highlights blind spots.

2. **They have a commitment to continuous learning.** Members are committed to moving forward and growing, both professionally and personally. They recognize that they don't have all the answers and that there's always room for growth. They're open to different ways of thinking and are willing to put in the work necessary to improve. They bring new ideas and thoughts to the group.

3. **They stand with other members.** Members should be honest with each other, even when someone makes a bad decision or messes up. Members pick each other up and want each other to win. They celebrate successes and learn from their own and others' failures. Members don't judge each other's mistakes; they seek to understand and support.

4. **They are accountable.** Members are honest. They don't rubber-stamp anything. If they don't believe something is the right thing to do, they speak up. They also don't stand by and accept undesirable behavior or conversations or wait for someone else to deal with it. They hold each other accountable for the guidelines set by the group, commitments they make to each other, and progress.

5. **They have abundance thinking.** Members are committed to making themselves available to each other. They're there when needed, and they're responsive. They give first without expecting anything in return.

6. **They know how to be vulnerable.** Members unpack weaknesses, failures, and insecurities and are generous listeners when others do the same. There are no secret pockets (i.e., something kept close to the vest and rarely discussed, frequently involving withholding information crucial to the conversation for fear of being judged or embarrassed). Shortcomings are acknowledged.

These attributes take different lengths of time to develop, and some are more easily cultivated than others. However, the group will only be as strong in each characteristic as its weakest member is. For example, vulnerability is the hardest to achieve for all members equally. Individuals have different levels of how vulnerable they're willing to be. So the group will only be as vulnerable as a whole as the weakest member allows. Some members will be extremely vulnerable, and that will help the others move up the scale, but it may take more time than you think for that to happen. Vulnerability is something you cannot rush or manufacture. But when you witness members being vulnerable, it's magic.

An exercise I like to do every year or so with a group is to ask them to rank themselves on each characteristic on a scale of 1 to 5. We discuss where they're low and where they're open to shifting. Then they rank the group on a scale of 1 to 5. After that ranking, we all discuss where improvement can be made individually and as a group. This exercise is very impactful in improving their performance and their connection and cohesion.

An Advanced Exercise for Groups Already with Guidelines

The more the above attributes are developed, the more likely members will bond and stay together. They begin to experience something they cannot live without—and don't want to live without. Your goal is to have the member consider their dues a must-have in their budget and strategic plan each year. It becomes a part of their strategy for growth, risk management, learning, and innovation—again, the French Laundry experience.

Hard guidelines, on the other hand, take the form of tangible action that can be easily seen and experienced. For example:

- Be on time for meetings.
- Attend 80 percent of all meetings in a year.
- Respond to peer inquiries in a timely fashion.
- Be present during meetings—no phone calls or emails unless there's an emergency.
- Don't tell but offer experiences and perspectives.
- Share all relevant information about your situation. Be as vulnerable as possible.
- Keep commitments and make progress.
- Let the moderator know in advance if you need to be absent or are running late.
- Keep all discussions and documents confidential (and as the moderator, make sure everyone signs a nondisclosure document).
- Mentor a new member.
- Be an accountability partner to another.
- Be willing to meet a prospect or attend a sample meeting.
- Make an effort to generate referrals.

- Prepare an annual presentation or any other reporting commitment.
- Share financials. (This may be optional for your groups.)

Note the difference: soft guidelines are values that are illustrated by behaviors, and hard guidelines are actions you take that support the structure of the meetings. When you put soft and hard guidelines together, you have a gauge of the emotional intelligence, EQ, of a member as well as the PaC as a group. The goal is to get the group to embrace and master all the guidelines, and there will always be members with impeccable behavior who rise to the level of mentors. You shouldn't be the only one modeling the guidelines.

If you're wondering about in-person versus virtual guidelines, in concept, they're the same, but there will be a few nuances in hard guidelines. For example, a virtual norm might have the following:

- Raise your hand when you want to speak.
- Mute if there is excessive background noise, or use unmute to signal when you have a comment or are ready to speak.
- Use chat for certain situations (e.g., giving feedback, nudging a member to wrap up, etc.).
- If we need to move on, a white flag will be waved.
- Stay focused and present on screen; don't do email or multitask.
- Close all tabs on your computer to reduce distraction.
- Be in an environment that's confidential, void of noise and interruptions.
- Video is to be on at all times (with exceptions for small moments of time).

A Deeper Dive into the Benefits of Guidelines

Guidelines positively impact you as the moderator as well as all of your members. The key benefit for you is that the group is easier to moderate, and here are some reasons for that:

- The members know what's expected of them, which means you spend less time coaching them as undesired behavior occurs.
- It's less stressful for you and for them when you've been proactive about what's expected of them as members, as you can refer back to the behavior agreed to when correction is needed.
- Adding the right-fit member to the group has a higher success rate when there are guidelines to reference in the selection process. If a prospect doesn't want to commit to the guidelines, you know they won't be a good member.
- Group participation is elevated so that you're able to moderate at a higher level, making it more enjoyable for you and improving your skills and personal development.
- There's a feeling that comes with a PaC built on a solid foundation of agreed-upon behavior. It feels like a team in sync.
- The member experience is heightened as well, and here's how:

  - They understand what ideal behavior looks like, and they constantly practice it, making the meeting more effective and efficient.
  - They become better members, supporting each other by modeling the behaviors.
  - A higher level of trust is created when everyone knows what's expected of them.

- There's a sense of ownership and deeper connection because of norms established.

- Questions about behavior are removed, which alleviates the stress that comes with trying to figure out how to act in a meeting.

- Members will receive a higher return on their investment of time since you'll be able to conduct a more meaningful meeting. There's no time spent talking about how people need to behave.

How to Create Guidelines

If I want buy-in from you about going out to dinner, what's one thing I could do? Ask you where you'd like to go. I've instantly engaged you. It shouldn't surprise you, then, to find out that moderators don't go into their PaC meetings with established guidelines. Instead, they co-create the guidelines with the members. You're much more likely to follow guidelines you had a hand in writing.

When starting a new group, introduce the idea of guidelines by pointing out that the group is, at that point, a clean slate. Together, and with your guidance, they'll articulate what good behaviors look like. This is a necessary step in illustrating the formality of the experience they're about to embark on. Your group will appear more professional and will operate with intention because you've underscored the importance of the MX by taking the time to create the guidelines as a group.

Know that you might also need to reiterate the guidelines or even revise them if the group has adopted less-than-desired behaviors. These behaviors can look like this:

- Developing a habit of arriving late, leaving early, or being absent
- Interrupting conversations
- Responding to email or typing on a laptop
- Asking for conversations to be repeated because they weren't listening
- Offering ideas or solutions too early in the process due to impatience or laziness
- Not preparing COPIs or never having any
- Not following through on a commitment made to others in the group
- Not making progress on their own issues or problems (the P and I in COPI)

Finally, guidelines can be used with high-functioning groups as a way to nudge them toward operating at an even higher level. There's no such thing as no room for improvement. Shaking things up a little to keep people on their toes so they aren't complacent is sometimes a skillful strategy for improvement.

There are slight differences in the instructions for creating guidelines, depending on whether the group is new, already has guidelines, or is advanced.

For New Groups with Founding Members

First, have your thoughts outlined. Think about what would be or has been essential for successful PaC experiences. Next, during the group's first meeting, ask the founding members to brainstorm and add their insights. *What's important to them? What do they expect from themselves and each other?* This will create ownership and excitement, bonding your members to the group and to your process. After discussion and agreement, create a document or visual of the guidelines for reference at each meeting. They'll become a charter for the group and the beginning of creating the culture you desire.

For Existing Groups with or without Defined Sets of Guidelines

Ask the group what they think their group norms are. *What normal behaviors are showing up regularly? What behaviors do they like, want to get rid of, want to change, and want to add?* Have them brainstorm what behaviors they personally need from their peers and from you to have the best experience possible. Then brainstorm what behaviors they believe they need to improve upon to make the experience better for their peers.

At some point, existing groups that have been together over time should revisit and evaluate their guidelines. Some guidelines become out of date for where the group is operating, and others need to be added. This is most true with hard guidelines. Particularly enlightening is evaluating how well they're performing with the soft guidelines.

The advanced exercise I referenced earlier is to take the guidelines created by the group and the characteristics of a high-functioning group mentioned earlier and ask every member to quietly reflect and rank how well the group as a whole is doing on each one and then rank how they personally are doing on each one. Two rankings emerge to then discuss openly. Publicly identify which items need to be improved upon or changed entirely. Then have each member choose the soft area they're committed to improving. Usually, most members choose number eight (vulnerability).

Once the exercise is over, always memorialize it by creating an updated document for reference. Consider having everyone sign it as their commitment to each other and themselves.

Now that we've clarified how best to design the initial experience for your members, let's get into the formula I've developed that's at the heart of hundreds of transformative meetings.

Takeaways

- Creating an MX makes you money and differentiates you.
- MX starts when the prospect says yes!
- Always do an Orientation.
- Guidelines make your moderating role easier and elevates the MX.

Resources

Use the QR code at the back of the book to access the

- Guideline template, and
- Member Journey Maps.

CHAPTER 5

The Formula for Successful Meetings

I define a successful meeting as one in which all of the members have an extraordinary French-Laundry-type experience. This means they not only get their unique needs met, but they also get value beyond anything they could get on their own, including perspectives they hadn't even thought of. If I'm doing my job right in educating you and then you do yours for your PaCs, people will say there's something special about your PaCs and that they're so "next level." Imagine having a waiting list for your PaCs. Imagine retaining your members for years. This scenario doesn't happen by accident. There's a formula for successful meetings, and it's rooted in having a solid, purposeful structure that's implemented in a way that's fluid and intentional.

This chapter will explain the *Why* of meeting structure, then will describe my four-step *How* of successful meetings. The *Why* and the *How* of *moderating* are so important that the following chapter will be devoted entirely to them. No amount of impressive moderating will compensate for a meeting without a plan or a meeting without consideration of the unique needs of the people in the room. Let's get into why that is.

Why Is *Why* So Important?

When you know the Why behind an action, that underlying motivating helps you learn, retain, and execute. Answers to Why questions orient you to the theory behind what you're doing so you can be consistent and efficient. The Why is like your North Star, reminding you of where you want to be and guiding you. And having an understanding of why things happen better equips you to handle the unexpected when it occurs. When you've addressed someone's Why for an experience, you're setting the stage for an extraordinary experience.

Why Is Meeting Structure So Important?

The last fifteen years have demonstrated to me that a lack of meeting structure is one of the main reasons a member will leave your PaC.

> **A lack of meeting structure is one of the main reasons a member will leave your PaC.**

Structure is the foundation for your agenda—its bones. Without proper structure, meetings can become chaotic because they lack direction. Expectations about what topic to raise and when won't be clear, and overall, the experience will be frustrating for everyone involved. Busy leaders won't tolerate meetings that waste their time or don't add value. Additionally, they won't waste time in meetings if the right people aren't present. This is also why having the right peers together, as discussed earlier, is critical to success.

The quality of your life is a direct reflection of the expectations of your peer group. Choose your peers wisely.

—TONY ROBBINS

Structure sets the stage for the type of meeting you'll have. For example, if a priority of your members is accountability, then your structure has to have trigger points for accountability. If education is critical to your members' growth, then your meeting's structure will incorporate continuous learning and reflection. If insights and problem-solving are the priorities, then structure your meeting around them. Before you create your agenda, which will include how much time to allot to the four steps of successful meetings, you must first know what's most important to the group. Once you have that information, you can reverse-engineer your agenda. Note that the amount of time for each step will vary in each meeting to accommodate the needs of your PaC. And it's even more common that *during* your meeting, you'll adjust the amount of time in each section due to the unexpected needs of the group at that particular moment.

Structure or Consequences

From a moderator's perspective, a clear structure is the path to making certain your priorities are addressed during the meeting. That path needs to have markers that tell you what should be happening and where you are in your journey toward your outcomes. After all, how will you know you're on the right track for the results your members expect if you don't have that kind of structure?

The intention of a PaC meeting, in my mind, is results and insights. The outcomes are clear and tangible, not wishy-washy. For example, productivity is a frequent topic. Leaders are always trying to figure out how to be more productive. Being a member of a PaC, *your*

PaC, should increase productivity for these leaders because having ten-plus smart, unbiased peers around a table is better than having only your own head. But this only happens if there's structure.

> Martha was a CEO who was referred to me. She had a dissatisfying experience as a member of a competing peer group. I called her to learn why she was considering leaving her group. Why did she want to speak with me? When I posed the question to her, a lengthy hesitation followed, and then, rapid fire, she mentioned lax meetings, irrelevant conversation, staying on a topic too long, and slow, unstimulating conversation. She paused, and in a very deliberate way, she said, "The only way I know to explain this to you is I was looking for a wow experience, and I didn't get it."

Without asking for her definition of a "wow experience," I got it; I immediately understood what she meant in light of her previous, rapid-fire remarks. "What you're saying is that you want to walk out of a meeting and have gained so much value that you say, 'Wow, that was worth my time today. Of all the other things I could have done, that was the best use of my time.'"

Martha became a member of one of my councils and remained one for years. She attributes her rise in satisfaction to the structure of the meetings. Structure is the only way to ensure that members like Martha walk away with valuable insights *every time*. Without a process, it's always a gamble.

After analyzing my most successful PaC meetings in search of common denominators, I created a four-step process to duplicate my prior successes. I've been teaching it to other moderators for years, and each time we get to this part in the curriculum, new moderators are shocked by the level of detail I include. On the other hand, seasoned moderators immediately understand and appreciate the depth.

My recommendation for the following steps is to use them, in order, every time (there will be a rare exception), but to customize the amount of time you spend on each according to the needs of your group. No two meetings look exactly the same if the moderator is paying attention to what each member needs that day.

4 STEPS TO SUCCESS

1 *OPENING – SET THE TONE*

2 *MEMBERS DON'T KNOW WHAT THEY DON'T KNOW . . .*

3 *MEMBERS KNOW WHAT THEY DON'T KNOW . . .*

4 *WRAP-UP*

Step 1: The Opening

The opening of a meeting sets the tone of the whole meeting experience:

- A dynamic opening sets the tone for a dynamic meeting.
- A late opening sets the tone of being behind already—a lackadaisical approach.
- An upbeat opening means an upbeat meeting can be expected.

- An unorganized opening translates to: an unorganized meeting is on the way.

While the opening doesn't always foreshadow how the meeting will go, it definitely sets the tone and the pace. In other words, it sets expectations and informs the perceptions that members will have. You can influence both of those, and you should do what you can to manage them.

Five Keys to an Extraordinary Opening

1. **The physical setup.** It establishes the mindset for the meeting and gets everyone settled. For example, a circle sends a different message (inclusive) from a classroom arrangement (training). A boardroom-style meeting means business and professionalism. If you're virtual, your background is very important, as is your lighting.

2. **Announcements.** If there are any housekeeping items, such as the following month's meeting logistics or the status of absent members that month, taking care of that up front is something I recommend. Members want to know why someone is missing or if they are running late. This also gives your members a few moments to get to their seats if running behind, finish a conversation, and get organized for the meeting to start. That means the slightly late arrivals are missing the least important part of the meeting. The heavy-lifting thinking starts with MyTransition™ (the next key), so announcements are a "warm-up" of sorts for everyone. If you wait until the end of the meeting for announcements, they might not happen. There's usually an engaging discussion occurring, and you might have to cut it short for the announcements or punt them because you don't want to

interrupt the conversation. Neither is optimal, and both put you in an undesirable position as a moderator.

3. **My Transition.** This is my term for transitioning the mindset of the participants to the purpose of the meeting. You want them to become present as soon as possible. During years of moderating meetings, I've observed that members, especially CEOs, can take twenty, thirty, or even sixty minutes to settle in. Some remain in tactical mode, addressing their daily responsibilities, putting out last-minute fires, and even taking one last phone call. Within a four-hour meeting, even twenty minutes is too much time to waste.

When I talk about transition time, I use the analogy of going on vacation. How many days does it take before you assume the vacation mindset? If you're someone who takes a few days, it's entirely possible that once you settle in, you realize you don't have much time left! How much better could your experience be if you learned how to get into your vacation mindset faster?

I've learned that quick adoption of the PaC meeting mindset is positively correlated with a member's overall meeting experience. This means moving from tactical to strategic thinking as soon as possible: working *on* rather than *in* their business. It's difficult to change perspectives when your mind is still on daily business concerns. To help shift the thinking of members, I take them through a brief but effective and intentional exercise at the start of each meeting that shows where they currently are in their business, professionally and sometimes personally. It's like a dashboard, and I get to it via prompts or questions to consider.

- *Prompt 1:* Describe your mindset in one or two words. *Why?* It causes them to take stock of what's going on with them at the moment and think about it. You're bringing them to the present, and whatever they answer tells you about their state of mind and what you need to be prepared for from them during the meeting. Their answer tells you what they need from the meeting, and from you, that day.

- *Prompt 2:* Ask a question directly related to the group and the theme of the meeting that day. *Why?* Their answer gives you insight into their business that you might not otherwise get. This question can also be both fun and silly to provide an opportunity for bonding.

  □ How do you choose a question? Think about what will give you information *the member can use* at that moment. For example, let's say members are having a hard time retaining talent. You might ask:

  □ What's your best retention tool for employees?

  □ What tactics do you use to create happy, productive employees?

  □ What's the number-one reason for attrition *that you can't seem to fix?*

  □ How do you know when an employee is at risk of leaving?

By using one of these prompts, not all of them, you not only help members transition into the meeting in a deeper way, but you also simultaneously surface potentially valuable information for everyone present. Again, just by being present at the meeting and listening, members benefit from the PaC, *if the moderator knows what they're doing.*

4. **Accountability.** Get updates from the members in a controlled way by asking about the status of the commitments they made in the previous meeting. Ask for updates from those you processed COPIs with during the previous meeting.

5. **COPIs.** Identify the topic that needs to be addressed by asking each member, "What COPI do you have today?" It's important to ask the question expecting each member will have a COPI. If you ask, "Who has a COPI today?" two things will happen: (1) you get crickets, or you only get COPIs from members prepared to speak up, and (2) you won't get COPIs from those members who want to just pass that day or haven't put enough thought into it. This can ultimately result in a member going months without ever mentioning a COPI. That's a red flag the member might be resigning, as I'll discuss later. Your objective is to hear what each member's COPI is because every member has one. Always. *If they've thought about it.* If they haven't, they're essentially saying it's not important enough, it's too scary, or it's too difficult. The most skillful way to handle this will be explained in the following chapter. For now, remember that part of the reason they're in your PaC to begin with is to think hard about their challenges, opportunities, problems, or ideas. If they're not doing that, you need to find out why. The decision about whose COPI to prioritize, because you can't process them all, will be based on who has the greatest need at the moment. You and the group decide this together. Finally, avoid having a member go into detail about their COPI during MyTransition. Keep the detail to the COPI part of the agenda; otherwise, valuable time is wasted repeating it.

Step 2: Members Don't Know What They Don't Know

In the 1970s, Noel Burch devised the **Stages of Competence Model** to describe what happens when we learn new skills. His four stages, which have been variously renamed, refer to (1) not knowing what you don't know, (2) knowing what you don't know, (3) knowing how to do your new activity or use your new knowledge and being aware of it, and (4) knowing how to do your new skill so well that you're not thinking about all of the various steps.

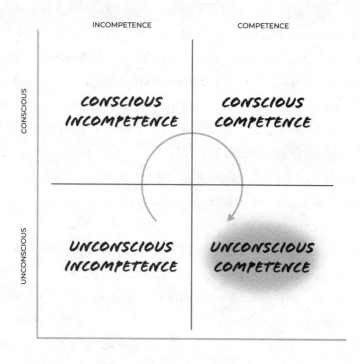

Burch's name for *You don't know what you don't know* was "unconscious incompetence." Unconscious incompetence comes into play in step 2 with the *Perspective Report™*, which is like a member spotlight: a time in the agenda when a member presents about their business to their group of peers using a format the moderator has prescribed.

The Perspective Report™ is an incredible tool that provides a unique opportunity for the member to consider where they are (in life and business), how they got there, and where they are going. The tool explores the individual's life from their most impactful life events to their weakness and fears. Almost equally as valuable, the tool helps to create deep relationships within the group in a way that makes the other members want to support the individual in more meaningful ways, and creates trust (and even love) for the individual in their new group.

—KEVIN DELL'ORO, THE BAINBRIDGE GROUP;
CERTIFIED LICENSED PARTNER, ANNAPOLIS

My format is called the *Perspective Report*; it's their perspective on their business. During each monthly meeting, one member presents either their strategic plan or an overview of their business using the Perspective Report. Usually, each member presents once a year. It's ideal if they include

- the personal aspects of their FORD,
- how they started their business,
- why they started their business,
- their values,
- triumphs and pitfalls in the past,
- where the business is currently,
- ideas about future trends,
- key performance indicators (KPIs),
- objectives and key results (OKRs), and
- exit strategy.

This is the opportunity for the rest of the group to raise issues and opportunities they see that perhaps the member hadn't thought about. In other words, *the member doesn't know what they don't know*; they don't see it. But thanks to this scheduled, intentional time, their peers can help them see what they're missing. It's also an exceptional opportunity for the members to learn a great deal about the member presenting. As a result, their future input to the presenting member will be more relevant.

Step 3: You Know What You Don't Know

In each PaC meeting, members can present their COPI, which is a thoughtful process that helps them move beyond obstacles and explore the viability of opportunities. The COPI process represents conscious incompetence because the member knows what they don't know or what they need because they are bringing the topic up. They are aware.

Here's how it works: After step 2 (in other words, part of moderating is making sure members don't bring up their COPIs when they feel like it, and if they do, you gently tell them that the COPI has its own designated time), one at a time, members present their COPIs. They must clearly describe why it's important to them, what (if anything) they've done in the past, what they are considering doing, and what they want their peers to address.

> **The COPI process represents conscious incompetence because the member knows what they don't know or what they need because they are bringing the topic up.**

This process ensures members understand the issue and what is being asked of them. It requires thought, consideration, and preparation on the member's part, but all that work helps the member because it provides them with clarity about their own situation. Members frequently discover that the challenge or opportunity isn't what they originally perceived it to be. For the best results, a member should plan and think about their issue before the meeting versus at the meeting on the fly. Providing them with a cheat sheet to use is very helpful.

The COPI process is all about structure, which prevents valuable time from being wasted. Members should spend 20 percent of their time talking and 80 percent of their time listening. Valuable meeting time shouldn't be wasted because a member is unsure of what they want from their peers. The other members shouldn't have to waste their time with needless questions to understand the issue at hand. That's why it's helpful for members to think in advance about what their COPI would be that day. When someone has sufficiently defined their needs and explained their situation, insights from their peers will follow.

Here's what step 3 looks like in practice:

- While a member is speaking or posing a question, no one should interject or ask questions. Interruptions pull the member's dialogue off course, and eventually, the entire meeting can lose its structure. Normally 15 percent of the total time spent on the member's COPI is in this stage.
- Once the member has exhausted all points in their COPI presentation:

  - Their peers ask questions for clarity. At this stage, *members refrain from trying to solve the problem.* Solving too early often results in poor advice given because conclusions and assumptions were made before all the data was presented. This stage represents the most time— usually 70 percent of the allotted COPI time is spent on questioning.

- After all questions have been asked, the members take a few moments to quietly develop their recommendations.

- After that brief time (a few minutes), all members share their thoughts. Even if a member doesn't think they have something to offer, they do. They always have opinions or thoughts, and it's their job at this point to voice them. This stage represents the remaining 15 percent of that member's COPI process.

- Note that sometimes recommendations invite more questions. That's perfectly fine, as they often bring further clarity to the issue. But it should be limited. If it happens frequently, then the group needs to work on being better questioners. You can help them with this in two ways: lead by example and show them how to be better at questioning, or do a working session on the importance of helpful questioning. You can download my resource on "The Power of a Question" at the link provided at the end of this chapter.

Once the question-asking process is complete, the member posing the question considers the feedback and whether they want to use all or part of it to solve their problem or address their opportunity. They don't need to decide on the spot, because accountability will happen in the next meeting, when they'll be expected to give an update. The member is also not to debate the feedback but instead to take it all in. This isn't a time for banter; it's a time to listen and understand the feedback.

With all of this said, one of the indications that a PaC is secure and supportive and very connected is when a member tells another member they need to talk about something. This situation occurs in high-functioning PaCs where one member calls out the unconscious incompetence of another member. This is done in a kind and compassionate manner, and good moderator skills are crucial (this is discussed more in the following chapter). Essentially, one member believes their colleague isn't addressing an important situation because they're avoiding it, they're totally blind to it, or they see it but don't think it's a big deal. That's not a fun message to hear or to deliver. But when it's done right—when members bring up COPIs of their peers—they're helping them shift from unconscious incompetence to conscious competence, and that's a measure of how well they know each other and care for each other.

*Noel Burch Model with LXCouncil Meeting Structure

Step 4: Wrap-Up

Just as how you open the meeting sets the tone for the meeting, how you wrap it up sets the tone for how *your members* view the time they just invested with you.

The wrap-up contains two important elements: *gain commitment* and *gain value. Gain commitment* refers to members committing to do something to accelerate themselves forward prior to the next meeting. The objective is to allow them to identify—out loud—the one thing they want to focus on. It should be the one thing that means the most to them to make progress on: their priority. Capture that commitment so you can reference it in the next meeting for accountability. Sometimes we call this their unbreakable commitment. Notice we don't use the word *goal.* We do this because commitments are less likely to be missed than goals, even SMART (specific, measurable, achievable, realistic, timely) goals. Commitments tend to speak more to who you are and what motivates you. Furthermore, it's not unusual for members to change goals as they get closer to the time they allotted because they desire bigger goals, move the goalpost, or are focusing on something totally different now.

> **Commitments are less likely to be missed than goals, even SMART (specific, measurable, achievable, realistic, timely) goals.**

Gaining value must be done last, and is where the epiphanies usually arise. Ask the members for their one *aha* moment. What was their most valuable takeaway from that meeting? The answer they give you is the value they received from the meeting. Hearing every member's answer validates the worth of the meeting and solidifies why they're a member. The answers are also a powerful learning tool for you, as your members have just validated your work as well as told you what's important to them. Gaining value ends the meeting on a high note. It's the last thing etched in their minds as they depart. Don't you want them thinking of the value as they leave the meeting? Their French Laundry experience!

Better Practices

There are moments and topics that reliably arise during the planning of your meetings or the moderating of the meetings. I'll leave the How of moderating to the next chapter, but there are a few procedural questions with regard to your role as moderator. Let's address these common pain points and questions.

Are There Times I Meet with Members Individually?

Private meetings between the moderator and each member are a standard part of the membership package. I call them Quarterly Achievement Sessions (QASs), and they're usually held between group meetings. It's important to define this structured time. It's not a coaching session (and the next chapter will get into why), designed to get the client to arrive at their own answers. It's also not a 1-2-1 (abbreviated 121 in the industry) check-in conversation that doesn't have a defined structure. I think a bit of history will best explain what they are and why I created them.

One of the ways many moderators struggle with scaling groups is that they spend an inordinate amount of time coaching members one on one (i.e., having 121s). Back in 2012, I was one of those moderators, burned out by doing 121s. And like many moderators, I wasn't trained to do coaching. However, I was trained that coaching sessions were necessary for member retention. Meanwhile, my members were saying they didn't need them or like them or have time for another meeting. I agreed, and I sought to find something better and test if retention increased or decreased with my new way. Well, it increased! And by more than 10 percent. And my personal ROI increased by more than 25 percent. What was my new way? The QAS.

What is the QAS exactly? It's a Quarterly Planning Session to review your member's achievements that are results of being a member. You review the last ninety days of achievement and value-add received, both in the business and as a leader. Then together you look forward and plan the next ninety days of their membership, prioritizing COPIs, helping them plan their Perspective Report, and proactively addressing concerns, member behavior, etc.

As a result, you've acquired a lot of important intel for planning your next ninety days' worth of agendas. For example, which members will need extra time for important COPIs? Do you have the peace of mind that comes from knowing the members presenting their Perspective Reports are prepared? Do you know if you should get a speaker and what their topic would be, and are you due for a roundtable discussion? The QAS always helped me head off a possible termination, validated what members valued, gained me referrals, and provided valuable feedback about my moderation. Quarterly Achievement Sessions were a game changer regarding positive impact on the MX, my time, and my financial return.

Should I Have Speakers at My Meetings?

Peer advisory council meetings should always be geared toward the members—their businesses, their goals, and their challenges. Because of possible unnecessary distractions, you have to be very careful when inviting guest speakers to meetings. Finding one speaker whose words are relevant and meaningful to every member is rarely easy.

Typically, speakers at business-group meetings present a concept or idea that's trending in the business world. Unfortunately, that message doesn't always relate to an individual business's strategy, culture, or organizational structure at that moment. Be wary of trendy messages and ideas that present one-size-fits-all strategies, as they frequently set your members back rather than moving them forward.

By no means am I saying you shouldn't have outside speakers. Once again, my message is to be intentional and protective of your members. Just because you know a great speaker doesn't mean you should have them at your meeting. If you were a paying member of your group, what kinds of speakers would *you* find valuable? What speakers would *you* pay to listen to?

For any prospective speakers, vet their presentations to be sure they cater to the level of sophistication of your members, they're content-rich, and they hit upon points that are relevant. And don't allow blatant selling; your members don't want to be sold to in a meeting they're paying for. Remember to give the members the option to contact the speaker directly.

What's the Best Time to Do the Agenda?

Always do your next month's agenda immediately after your meeting. *Why?* The agenda includes what needs to happen, what topics will be discussed or followed up, accountability, member spotlight, and info on the speaker if you have one. All of that information is top of mind right after a meeting. What you don't know you can fill in later, but doing your agenda immediately after a meeting allows your mind to let it go. If you don't, you'll think about it all month. So get everything documented immediately, from commitments to COPI follow-up, to actions you need to do like sending out an article, etc., without fear of losing your notes or forgetting exactly what was meant by your handwriting. Having the agenda done or almost done immediately after your meeting for the next meeting will give you peace of mind.

SAMPLE AGENDA

Opening

- *ANNOUNCEMENTS*
- *MY TRANSITION* ™
- *ACCOUNTABILITY*
- *IDENTIFY + PRIORITIZE COPIs*

Member Presentation

MEMBER SPOTLIGHT
OR
PERSPECTIVE REPORT ™

COPI Processing

Wrap Up

- *GAIN COMMITMENT*
- *GAIN VALUE*

How Do I Deal with Confidentiality?

Confidentiality shouldn't be assumed; it needs to be talked about and agreed to. Having the words *confidential* or *confidentiality* posted in your meeting room reminds the members of their obligation to each other in and outside the meeting. If you print an agenda, have the words watermarked on it or in bold at the bottom or a reminder in your opening remarks. This is particularly important if a member is handing out confidential information such as their strategic plan or financials. If your meeting is virtual, verbally remind members or include "Confidential" on any documents shared in advance or presented on your screen. The importance of defining and emphasizing confidentiality at each meeting cannot be overstated. Not all members will truly understand the depth of what confidentiality means. Here's how you might do that:

> **The true definition of confidentiality is that nothing is talked about or referenced outside the meeting unless it's between members.**

- Have each member explain what confidentiality means to them.
- Have each member indicate their biggest fear of confidentiality being broken.
- Give scenarios of when confidentiality is critical, such as acquisitions, personnel changes, partner issues, large customer challenges, and financials shared.
- Ask the group if it's OK to share who's in the group publicly.
- Ask the group what breaching confidentiality would look like.

The true definition of confidentiality is that nothing is talked about or referenced outside the meeting unless it's between members. Be sure your group really knows the definition of confidentiality and what it means to their participation by talking through the above questions. It's a better practice to have the group articulate it and create the definition themselves. Nothing tells it better than citing examples of how to handle those situations.

Should I Take Notes during the Meeting, and If I Do, Should I Share Them?

If you choose to take notes, I recommend never publishing them for two reasons:

1. You put yourself and the group at a liability risk, as well as breach of confidentiality, if the notes are incorrect or misleading. Notes are paper trails that can be left on a desk, visible in a trash can, or otherwise find their way into the wrong hands. You don't want to be responsible for that. Remember, you're not an official board of directors with fiduciary obligations that require note-taking.

2. Publishing notes doesn't enhance vulnerability. Many times your members won't want their conversations on the record. *Would you?* So take notes for yourself, and have your members take notes for themselves. And no one should be publishing their notes. This guidance is the same for virtual meetings and includes not recording the meetings as well.

If you're taking notes to share highlights and capture better practices and commitments, that's different. I'm referring to details that breach confidentiality. The key is for you and the members to be on the same page as to what's included in a summary document if you choose to do one.

Is There an Optimal Way to Set Up the Room?

For in-person meetings, set up the room to look like a boardroom, as that sets a tone of professionalism and indicates to your members that this is a serious time. Boardroom configurations signify that important topics will be discussed. The meeting room should have plenty of space to accommodate the chairs and table, and the temperature and lighting should be appropriate. Have water, handouts, name placards, paper, and anything else that will facilitate your members having a successful experience. You don't want any distractions, so think about the room for a moment from the point of view of a new member. What might be off-putting?

When it comes to seating, as a moderator you want to set your members up for success so there will be some strategy involved. For example, who should sit by whom?

- A new member is placed in the center of the group in their first meeting so they can feel included and embraced. If you place a new member on the outside or at the end of the table, they might feel excluded. Place a new member by their designated mentor if you assigned one, a familiar face, or someone they might already know. The goal is to make them feel at ease and as welcome as possible.

- Separate talkative members and members who have a tendency to do sidebar conversations. There's no need for you to have to moderate that behavior; let the seating do that for you.

- Place troublesome members next to you so you can easily and kindly moderate their bad behaviors. Sometimes placing them at the end of the table in direct eye contact with you works, as long as they'll look at you for clues and cues. I once had a member who rambled. We had an agreement that when I put my hand next to his, it was time to wrap up. While I thought it was our little secret, the rest of the group might have known. Regardless, it was a caring way to keep a member on track and in check. Find your style to do the same.

- Rotate members so they sit next to different members and get to know everyone. If members consistently sit by the same fellow members, a sense of comfort starts to set in. Comfort is not your friend when your goal is to increase the level of vulnerability and bonding in the group. I'll discuss this further in the next chapter.

What about Virtual Meetings? How Do You Set Them Up?

While you don't have the seating or room dynamics in a virtual environment, you do have choices that affect your member experience. First, choose the platform that's right for you. Research your options, and choose whatever level of technology that's appropriate for you and your members.

Remember that video builds trust, so you want to emphasize the importance of everyone having their cameras on the whole time. Without video, you don't know who else is in the room listening, and you don't know if the member is engaged and fully present. No video implies mystery rather than transparency, and there's nothing positive about that for a PaC meeting.

Also carefully consider how much and when you share your screen. Sharing your screen can cause everyone's faces to be minimized or disappear altogether. You want everyone to be able to see everyone for as much time as possible, as that's how you're able to best interact because you can see the expressions of others. It also helps people be present when they know everyone else can see their face.

How Much Do You Communicate Between Meetings?

There are two kinds of communication: *required* and *not required*. The only required communication is you sending meeting reminders. I send meeting reminders a week prior to the day, the day before, and the morning of the meeting. I recommend going beyond communicating the date, time, location, or video link.

What you say and how you say it plays a pivotal role in setting the tone and laying the foundation of the meeting. Feel free to let your personality shine here by being funny. Prepare the members by sharing the agenda in advance and mentioning anything you want them to think about, articles to read, videos to watch, etc. You know your members best. Will they even read your emails in time for the meeting or do any premeeting work? Plan your communication accordingly. I have a Licensed Partner, Henry, who's exceptional at writing reminder emails. His members read them, and I read them! They are funny, clever, and informative.

> *My notes to members include "dad joke" humor, themes about the time of year (such as May the Fourth, Star Wars Day), and often small jabs about funny moments from a recent meeting. Members will quickly progress to teasing and verbal jousting, which I am happy to include in my reminder emails and group updates.*
>
> —HENRY BASS, CEO OF AUTOMATION CREATIONS INC.;
> CERTIFIED MODERATOR, BLACKSBURG, VIRGINIA

As far as communication that isn't required, I encourage members to communicate with each other between meetings because it builds trust and camaraderie, and increases the value of membership. Communication might look like group emails with a member asking for a connection, a quick referral, feedback to check their thinking, or a real COPI that can't wait. Meeting each other for lunch, coffee, or a one-on-one call are all signs of a healthy group with members that genuinely respect and like each other. One way to cultivate this behavior is for you to *not* be the person the members go to for answers between meetings. Suggest they ask another member for input. When you guide members to reach out to their peers for support and expertise versus you alone, this enables your members to see how smart their peers are, increases vulnerability, breaks down barriers of judgment, and supports bonding.

Now let's get into the How *of moderating, and why it's very different from coaching, facilitating, or advising.*

 ## Takeaways

- Execute every agenda step, no matter how behind you might be. Even if all you spend on it is a few minutes.
- Meeting structure allows for members to go from unconscious incompetence to conscious competence.
- Never take confidentiality for granted.
- Ask for commitments, not goals.
- Gaining value is always last.

 ## Resources

Use the QR code at the back of the book to

- Download a sample agenda,
- Access the COPI Processing Cheat Sheet, and
- Download "The Power of a Question."

CHAPTER 6

What Does It Mean to Be a Moderator?

Why is this subject so important? Little has been written about it, and little is understood about what moderating really means. Most think that operating a peer group is all about the structure. And as we just discussed, structure *is* important, so people search for tips on setting up their group and think that's all there is. While you have to have good bones for the meeting, it's the skill of moderating that's underestimated. New moderators don't realize moderating is a profession, as there's no universal certification. But putting the learnings of this chapter into practice will be a game changer. Skill as a moderator distinguishes you from the pack of others running groups and gives you the same kind of confidence you feel after achieving a certification or degree. It's a calm but powerful feeling, knowing you can skillfully guide a peer group, nurturing their insights and helping them grow.

Again, I'll come back to the French Laundry experience. Having an unbelievable meal is expected, but what makes the experience memorable is how masterfully it's all delivered. If you compare this to the PaC experience, the meal is like the onboarding and processing of COPIs and QASs. You expect them to be part of the meeting. But it's the way of *being* of the server—their ability to be present and instantly know what your needs are, knowing when to stay silent and when to speak up—that makes the experience exquisite. Similarly, it's the way of being of the moderator that makes the experience rise above any other peer group meeting. This chapter will help you cultivate a way of being that makes your meetings run smoothly and maximizes insights and *ahas*. Your way of being includes the following:

- Presence—how can you be *in the moment*? And how do you balance being present with looking into the future to guide the meeting experience?
- What's the group's priority at any given moment, and what's the best way to make it known?
- What does each member need from the meeting, and how do you create the space to make it happen?
- How do you stay out of the "let-me-tell-you" mode of advising?
- How do you maximize the value from the group rather than from you?
- How do you manage the flow of a meeting so it appears organic?
- When do you speak, and why?
- What are your intentions for the meeting?

All of these will be addressed in this chapter, and you'll notice that the definition of *moderator* is what drives the answers. Once you understand the Why of moderating—what your job is and how it's different from facilitating, coaching, or consulting—the answers to the above questions should fall into place for you. Let's jump in!

The Moderator Role: What It Is and Isn't

What It Is

I define a moderator as one whose presence within the group is acknowledged by the group and whose actions are mostly transparent to the group. *Do you see what I did there?* The group knows who you are and what your title is. But how you're speaking, when you're speaking, and why aren't on the agenda necessarily. The moderator quietly encourages honest conversation while gently directing the group's dialogue toward leadership growth and personal learning. Members shouldn't have an experience of the moderator doing that; it's more like it just happens, from their perspective. The moderator's hand isn't at all heavy. Your responsibility as a moderator is to guide discussions and encourage ideas, openness, and debate. And beneath that guidance is an intention to reveal the variety of perspectives in the room. In order to be able to do this, as a moderator, there are some qualities you must have. As I describe them, I'll frequently mention what can happen if you do nothing, what new moderators do (basic move), and what seasoned moderators do (advanced move). Moderators must be:

> A moderator guides discussions with the intention to reveal the variety of perspectives in the room.

- **Knowledgeable about the type of group they're leading.** There's no need to be a subject matter expert, but you must have working knowledge about the group. *Why?* Because with that knowledge, you'll understand when it's time to wrap up a conversation or when it's time to allow a conversation to continue in more detail. Furthermore, you'll understand the jargon and nuances. When you know the level of importance and complexity of what's being discussed, you can moderate better. If you're lost in the discussion or you don't know what's important, then your focus is on keeping up and wondering what members are talking about rather than actually moderating.

- One dilemma that occurs if you're unaware of the nuances of your target market group is that you could expend a lot of effort with a PaC concept that's not ready for a peer group experience. I've seen moderators try to put together PaCs when the prospective members have no real experience to share. For example, start-ups—they're too green in business, and they're in survival mode. They're very tactical, and if you put a dozen of them in a group together, it would be the helpless being led by the clueless. They need something different because the peer group concept is too advanced for them. Your success, and your group's success, is contingent upon having a group of peers who are ready and able to participate in the PaC concept. Without that, you'll experience a false start.

  □ Basic move: You start with the traditional category of PaC, such as CEOs of diverse industries, meeting in person.
  □ Advanced move: Because you have direct experience with these leaders and have either been one yourself or worked with them for years, you can get more specific and narrow on your category—for example, CEOs of transportation companies meeting virtually.

- **Engaging.** Getting the entire group to participate in conversation equally is important for building diversity of opinion. You'll find your own style to pull information out of the ones who are quieter as well as a way to make the talkative ones aware. Your objective is to dial back the talkative ones and call on the nontalkative ones. When you allow a member to dominate the meeting because you don't know how to stop them, time is wasted, and both you and your members get antsy and impatient. This will frustrate the rest of the group and could be a reason why a member leaves. It's imperative to find your way to moderating through these moments. If engagement issues are recurring, you can address the behavior in your QAS, which is another reason that time with your member is invaluable.

  I've also observed moderators whose style is to say nothing for long periods of time. I'm talking about complete silence. But letting the group drift isn't moderating. Engaging means occasionally chiming in with a nudge for someone to speak or someone to stop speaking, moving the conversation along by simply saying, "OK" or "Good point" or nodding, or holding a finger up to prevent someone from interrupting an important point from being made.

  - ▫ Basic move: First, personally determine what type of signal or phrase you'll use to indicate it's time to wrap up and move on. For example, you might just chime in and say, "Thanks, Bob, for sharing those thoughts. I think the group needs to hear from Sandy [the not-talkative one or one who hasn't spoken yet]."

▫ Advanced move: Tell your group up front how you'll handle when it's time to move from one member talking to another. Use advanced signals (hands up, a yellow flag, standing up) or a phrase ("Thank you for the input," or "It's time to move on," or do something fun like call out an "ELMO," meaning "Enough; let's move on"). You'll maximize your time on only the most valuable discussions rather than on whatever discussions surface. I like to say that the goal of a meeting is to always move from one discussion to the next as the pinnacle of the discussion begins to wane. When you pivot to the next discussion at the right time, you avoid the point of diminishing return.

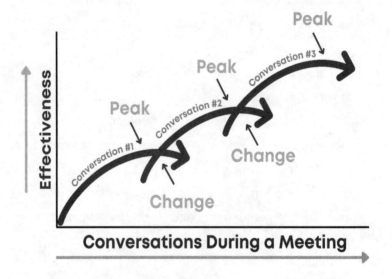

▫ Unless you feel you're contributing something that has a purpose and is advancing the conversation, don't take up space at the table. Strive to be talking for the good of the group—not to contribute just to contribute or to advance yourself.

- **Monitoring group dynamics at all times.** Moderators are always paying attention to what's going on with the group and each member. And if the dynamics need some gentle form of intervention or shifting, you must handle the moment. Handling the moment means taking stock of each member and gauging whether they're being present (not distracted by email, etc.) as well as if they're frustrated with the slow pace of conversation, have a look of confusion, are signaling they have questions, or are engaged with a look of agreement or disagreement (disagreement is engagement!). Any one of these requires you to intervene and give the member space to communicate or open a path (call on) for them to communicate. What you don't want to do is nothing and hope the members speak up themselves.

> Strive to be talking for the good of the group—not to contribute just to contribute or to advance yourself.

  - Basic move: Group callouts, during which you ask the group as a whole who has questions when you're not sure who does. You can also specifically ask whether the group is satisfied with the level of discussion and whether it's OK to move on.
  - Advanced move: Member-specific callouts. If a member has an inquisitive or confused look, stop and ask the member if they have a question or want further clarification. Be proactive. If members are impatient, however,

go ahead and move the meeting along; there's no need to ask questions.

- **Insight oriented.** Insights drive the results that produce *aha* moments. At the end of each meeting, as I'll discuss in a bit, each member should be able to articulate an *aha* moment. Those moments don't fall from the sky; they're cultivated throughout the meeting. Insights can come quickly, but they don't come from nowhere—they have a source. That source is the discussion during the meeting. And the way they grow and develop is through the moderator's use of illumination.
- If I were to distill moderation down to one word, I would choose *illumination.* Each step of the way during a meeting, each question, each decision you make should be in the service of guiding your members down a path of progressive learning. You're positioning them to discover how they got to where they are with their current COPI. As you do that, they experience insights into their situation.
- If you've done your job well, by the end of the meeting, they've had a series of discoveries that point to, or combine into, a bright moment of epiphany. They're hit with a sudden, thorough comprehension of their issue. It's a moment of deep learning for the member and a moment of real triumph for you as a moderator. These moments trigger both the intellect and the emotions of the member. They feel it as much as they "get it."
- Members might not see their epiphanies as they're building, but the moderator does. And the moderator nourishes the epiphanies as they're being constructed. By the end of the meeting, all that's left should be the member stating the

epiphanies out loud. But the moderator knows what was brewing the entire time, as they set the stage.

- Your goal as a moderator is to provide as much room for illumination in a meeting as possible. You can do this by encouraging reflection after a discussion and by insightful questioning.

The How of Illumination: Asking the Best Question in the Best Way at the Best Time

Leadership expert Michael J. Marquardt has said, "You don't have to have the answer to ask a great question. A great question will ultimately get an answer."[7] This is the epitome of the peer group value. The objective is to teach your members to be investigators and detectives—to be curious. You do this through open-ended questions, as they invite curiosity and exploration, unlike closed questions, which are limiting. The best open-ended questions start with *what, how, when, why, where,* *who, tell me more, what if,* or *I wonder.* Great questions benefit the member by challenging assumptions, changing points of view, stimulating creativity, engaging critical thinking, developing ownership of issues, and encouraging problem-solving. They allow members to see things differently in a fresh, unpredictable way that encourages breakthrough thinking and clarity. I call them Power Questions.

> **Teach your members to be investigators and detectives— to be curious.**

A simple way to get to a Power Question is to think of questions that are specific and bold, not general and generic. The more specific and bold the questions, the more specific and bold the answers.

---

7   Judith Ross, "How to Ask Better Questions," hbr.org (Harvard Business Review, March 28, 2017), https://hbr.org/2009/05/real-leaders-ask.

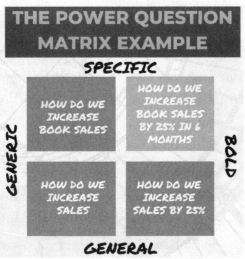

- Basic move: I always kept a list of the members' names beside me in the meeting, and I put a checkmark next to their name when I thought they had an *aha* moment or at least received an insight from a discussion. I was keeping track of the value they received, from my point of view. My objective was to be sure every member had a checkmark by the time Wrap-Up happened. And if the meeting was getting toward the end and someone didn't, I had to moderate to be sure the pending member received something of value that day. I did this by engaging them more. I'm not suggesting that everyone at every meeting should have *aha* moments, but they should all gain insight. The more you moderate, the more of them will happen because the group is getting more in sync and you're getting better at illumination. Remember that in closing you'll ask each member to articulate their insights—their takeaways. If they don't have one, don't let them off the hook. Ask them to reflect more and circle back.

- Advanced move: You're sure each member experiences *ahas* or insights. Throughout the meeting, you recap important discussions or COPI processing by asking each member what they received from that discussion. More skilled moderators can sense and see when a member has a look of epiphany. *What does that look like?* Usually, their eyes get bigger, they look like they're pondering a thought, and they actually say something like "Ohhhh, I get it now," especially after a Power Question was asked.

- Immediately following a Power Question is the perfect time to pause and ask the member what they're thinking. It gives them a moment to organize their thoughts and articulate them out loud, creating more stickiness for that moment of learning. You're creating time for them to briefly reflect, and the better you get at moderating and the more tightly run your meetings are, the more you will find moments to inject silent time for each member to think, sort their thoughts, and reflect. These moments are invaluable.

Once you have learned to ask questions—relevant and appropriate questions—you have learned how to learn and no one can keep you from learning what you want or need to know.

—NEIL POSTMAN, PROFESSOR AND AUTHOR

What Moderating Isn't

Understanding the misconceptions about moderating is vital for you so you can describe the difference to others. However, it's also vital because if you don't understand them, you might not be moderating, in practice, and if you're not, you're not going to produce the relationships, insights, and overall results PaCs were designed to achieve. A moderator is *not* the same as:

- **A coach.** Coaches maximize the potential of others through thought-provoking and creative processes. They don't give the answers, as they're not the expert on the client's topic. Coaching has a higher responsibility to each individual, even when the coaching is done in a group setting. A moderator, on the other hand, wants the experience and responsibility to the member to come from the member's peers.
- **An advisor.** Advisors have an area of expertise and can help in a specific way. And although the moderator might actually have the expertise a member needs, the moderator's job isn't to advise.
- **A mentor.** A mentor passes along knowledge and experience. They're a trusted guide who will share what they've learned. Moderators, however, don't share what they've learned as a matter of course. There might be appropriate times to do that, but it's not a defining part of the job.

- **A consultant.** Consultants are called upon for professional advice, technical advice, or their opinions. They're relied on to understand a problem and provide solutions. They don't look to develop your skills or performance but instead to use their knowledge to help you reach your goals. PaC members identify their own problems, and with the help of the group, they identify solutions. The moderator provides an environment where that can freely happen.
- **A facilitator.** I've heard plenty of people say that there's no difference between a moderator and a facilitator. If this reminds you of the peer group / Mastermind discussion, it's for good reason. And to make things more confusing, you'll hear the words *guide*, *chair*, and *leader* as well.

Just as with peer advisory council, I'll define it the way I use it so we're on the same page. Facilitators are:

- **Topic irrelevant** to whatever the meeting is about. In other words, they don't need to understand the business or industry of their client to lead the meeting.
- **Outcome centric,** as their goal is to help the group develop a plan and reach objectives as set by the client. They have an agenda designed to reach the expected outcomes.
- **Neutral** to the results. They have no vested interest and are unbiased.
- **Commanding.** They keep the participants focused and collaborating with dynamic conversation, and without getting off topic or tangential. They're focused on leading the discussions and agenda.

Facilitators develop and follow a plan that moves toward predetermined objectives set by a client. They aren't involved at all in the conversation among the members but are present to move it along and keep it on track. They lead the meeting. Now a moderator is also a leader of meetings, but they don't behave as the leader—they're the head, and it's obvious no one would be there without them, but they don't predetermine any outcomes. Moderators aren't shepherds of the meeting; they're architects of experiences that then take on a life of their own thanks to the environment.

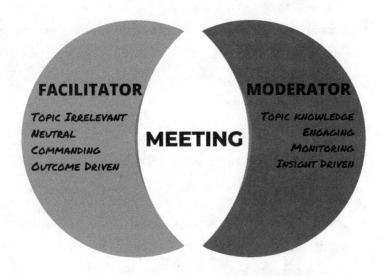

With all of this said, although the moderator's main role is to moderate, they go in and out of being a consultant, coach, collaborator, and facilitator as the moment requires. For example, after everyone has contributed to someone's COPI process, a better practice is for the moderator to provide their personal input. At that moment, they're stepping out of moderating and into a more wisdom-based role. And they can do that because their primary skill set is knowledge about the topic that's central to the group

> The philosophy of moderation is that it's not about you; it's about the group.

(unlike a facilitator). The philosophy of moderation is that it's not about you; it's about the group. You're moderating what the members are processing and creating clarity from that.

Required Soft Skills for Moderating

As you can sense from the discussion about illumination and Power Questions, moderating doesn't have a checklist for how, when, and why to listen, speak, or pivot. Although I'd love to say "When they say *X*, you say *Y*," and I'd love to give you scripts that will always work, I can't do that. *Why?* Because that would be irresponsible and disingenuous. Human interactions simply don't work like that. There are too many variables, many of which are invisible, such as what upsets an individual. You usually don't know the answer to that one until you accidentally bump into it.

What I can do, however, is tell you about the soft skills required to moderate at the highest level possible: emotional intelligence (EQ), vulnerability, team building, and confidence.

Emotional Intelligence, or Emotional Quotient

The ability to be diplomatic, empathic, collaborative, calm, respectful, and a good listener (soft skills), while simultaneously commanding accountability, discipline, focus, and inclusion (hard skills) is the optimal equation. As you might imagine, this sweet spot is tricky and requires being on point and aware of all visible dynamics at all times from your members. If you're thinking, *"That sounds exhausting!"* it is. You'll use a lot of brainpower to moderate your meetings, so don't be surprised if you're tired afterward.

Emotional Intelligence (EQ) is frequently used as an umbrella term for *soft* skills that are manifested in your way of being. There's a lot you can do, starting right now, to improve your EQ. Here are my top ten suggestions:

1. Respond instead of react. Observe how you respond or react to others and examine how your words and actions affect others. Be present, watch things unfold, and learn from them.
2. Listen actively.
3. Practice ways to maintain a positive attitude.
4. Take criticism well from your members.
5. Empathize with others. Be compassionate and kind.
6. Learn how to manage your emotions.
7. Embrace change.
8. Take responsibility for your actions.
9. Examine how your actions affect others.
10. Practice self-awareness.

That last one is huge. Why? Because self-improvement requires you to be self-aware. If you think about it, it's a necessary foundation for all of the other suggestions. But how do you know how you're progressing with your EQ if there's no one evaluating you? I created a *self-audit* for you to do after each meeting (there's a link to the download at the end of this chapter).

What should you be on the lookout for that speaks to your EQ? For the most part, anything that occurs in a meeting that you immediately have thoughts and feelings about is an opportunity to respond or react. It's your chance to speak or act from a place of wisdom. Or not. For example, when you disagree with something someone just said, check in with what you're thinking and feeling, and notice whether you're about to speak or act from that disagreement. Does it appear the other members are in disagreement as well? Someone with a high EQ doesn't react during disagreements. Instead, they consider what they should do or say and then they respond in a way that's best for the group rather than in a way that reveals how they really feel. Likewise, if your mood is off, you need to be aware of that and keep it in check. Even people who are constantly working on their self-awareness don't realize what's happening in every single moment. But if someone asks the right questions later, like with the *self-audit*, they might see things they missed.

Build Vulnerability

Vulnerability is usually thought of as being part of EQ. I've called it out separately because of its importance and difficulty to accomplish. I don't think moderating can be done well in its absence.

You either want to be vulnerable, or you don't. Brené Brown opened up the conversation around vulnerability with her TED Talk on "The Power of Vulnerability" in 2010. It's a staple in the peer group industry and a must-see for all moderators and, ideally, for members when they're ready. Moderators embody vulnerability and members aspire to it. Vulnerability shows up when you admit a mistake regarding the running of the group or regarding a decision that impacts the group. Moderators must lead by example. You set the tone.

Moderators must lead by example.

For instance, to model vulnerability during new-member introductions to the group, you might choose a few questions that are deeply revealing if answered honestly, such as these:

- What's one thing you're not proud of?
- What was the worst decision you ever made?
- What's your biggest regret?

- What part of your leadership style is holding you back?
- What are you most insecure about?

How much they want to disclose is up to them, but the more honest and open they are, the better it will be for them and for the group, as it gives the group the opportunity to support them.

As a moderator, part of your role is to bring vulnerability out in your members while not being completely vulnerable yourself. Remember, they're your clients—not your peers. Whatever level of vulnerability you reveal shouldn't cause them to question your ability, your skill set, or your judgment. Them being vulnerable with each other is the objective.

When you sense someone being vulnerable, support them and walk with them to see how far they will go. Encourage it. It reminds me of a saying: *When the student is ready, the teacher appears.* This is a metaphor for you as the moderator (teacher) being there to shepherd the member (student) when they're ready to take that step—that leap—to being more vulnerable. When someone shows up raw, which looks like pure emotion and real feelings, and expresses honest thinking, you lead with empathy, understanding, and relatability to open up more room for them to share.

Confidence

In addition to emotional intelligence and vulnerability, you need to have confidence in yourself as well as in the value of the PaC. Without confidence, you won't be able to close new members, conduct meetings with authority, or address member conflicts or poor behavior. Confidence will also help you instill the same in your members as they grow as leaders in their business because you'll be modeling it for them. They'll have confidence of their own to run their business!

Confidence develops along with competence. The better you get at moderating (or anything else), the more confident you become. Confidence is so important that I call it the number-one thing a moderator needs to protect. *What do I mean by that?* When you're not feeling confident, you have to act confident, regardless. Your lack of confidence is yours to deal with, not the group's, so you need to hide it from them. You also need to figure out what's causing your lack of confidence and then practice the skill set you're struggling with until you develop greater competence, which leads to confidence. What you absolutely cannot do is nothing. Finally, confidence doesn't include trying to impress your PaC. In fact, the less you try to impress the PaC, the more impressive you become.

Team Building

Building your PaC is like building a team—a team of peers who are better when together than they are on their own. They complement each other. There are differences between them in skill sets and experiences. There's diversity in past experiences, environment, how they grew up, their beliefs, and also how they're wired. All of these differences contribute to the different thinking present in the room.

Furthermore, there are synergies stemming from their strengths. Some members will be great with sales, some with operations, some with numbers, and some with people. Again, when they're all together, they complement each other and are stronger. You're building a dream team for your members, and because it's their dream team, it's also yours.

The Mindset of Successful Moderators

Mindset is a belief about yourself, a mental attitude, or a self-perception. There are five mindsets that successful moderators share.

1. **Seeking first to understand.** Successful moderators have a habit of *not* jumping to conclusions. Instead, they approach each moment with an attitude of curiosity and nonjudgment. I'm not saying anyone has this mindset perfected. At every meeting, you'll catch yourself making a judgment or jumping to a conclusion and then realizing you were wrong. I had a member who was late, again, and I was going to address it right then. I decided to sit back and see what happened instead. She proceeded to say she was notified that morning on her way to the meeting that her son's classmate had lice, and she was horrified. While driving to her PaC meeting, she rearranged care for her son, dropped him off at his grandmother's, arranged for medication to be administered just in case, and planned for how she would get her house disinfected if need be that day. And she did all of this in fifteen minutes! Instead of being upset that she was late and feeling disrespected, I felt admiration. You never know what a member is dealing with.

2. **Lifelong learning.** Some people are fine with what they know and don't seek out new topics to learn about or activities to learn how to do. Lifelong learners, however, have an insatiable curiosity. Your clients will likely be lifelong learners. That's one of the reasons they joined your PaC; they want to learn. Be current on the trends, innovations, challenges, and opportunities of the type of group you're leading. But also model being interested in a variety of topics. The more you grow, the more you bring to the group, and the more they will grow as a result. One of the biggest mistakes moderators make is to not grow themselves, and as a result, they become

outdated. As soon as you're outdated, your members know, and you're at risk for turnover.

3. **Confidentiality.** Do you know people who gossip—who reveal details of the lives of others they have no business revealing? That's the opposite of a confidentiality mindset. People who naturally have this mindset tend to be wonderful moderators because it's part of who they are to behave this way. Protecting privileged information is part of the duty of moderators. They don't share privileged information without permission. You should always ask for consent first if you feel others can benefit from sharing someone's information. And continuously remind the group, especially after a sensitive topic has been discussed or disclosed, that it shouldn't leave the meeting.

4. **Abundance.** People with an abundance mindset give first and give generously. They know how good it feels, and they never regret it. There will be many times you'll be faced with doing the right thing or not: whether to give of your time, money, expertise, or connections. Helping someone without the expectation of anything in return will build deeper relationships and loyalty. And that includes helping the group first. I've discussed selflessness before, and abundance is another way selflessness plays out. You'll be faced with deciding between something that's best for you or the group, and you should always choose the group. In the end, it's better for you.

When putting your first group together, for example, you might invite someone who's a perfect fit for the group but isn't in the position to pay, or maybe they can't pay the full amount. In this situation, you might postpone or reduce their payments short term so that the group gets to benefit from that person's participation. Notice I said short term. I'm not suggesting letting them participate for free—just that you consider creative possibilities and choose what's best for the group. Every time I've given first, I've always ended up ahead by receiving unexpected referrals, consulting engagements, and lifelong members.

5. **Meaningful relationships.** Successful moderators want relationships with their members that aren't transactional but are marked by genuine care and interest. These are critical for retention. You can't go wrong by being kind and genuine, remembering the FORD acronym from chapter 3 (family, occupation, recreation, dreams), and paying attention to details of the lives of your members. When you remember a date that's important to them, or check in after a critical meeting they had, or even remember their anniversary, it means a lot to them. You're demonstrating that you care.

The only caveat here is that if you're someone who's naturally drawn to others and wants to show you care, you may have noticed not everyone has the level of appreciation you would like for your intentions and actions. This is another instance where self-awareness and awareness of how others react to you becomes critical. People aren't the same. Some like to be texted, called, or emailed whenever you've got a thought to share with them. Others like that treatment but only from select people, and you might not be one of those people. And then there are the people who prefer limited communication with a limited number of people. The sooner you know where you stand with your members, the better your good intentions will come across. You can prevent miscommunication or inadvertently annoying someone if you make it a habit to ask during their Orientation meeting: *When I have something I'd like to share with you, do you prefer I text, email, or call you? And how would you like to share with me?*

The Moderator's Code of Conduct

There's a code of conduct that moderators follow while striving for excellence in this profession.

The list might appear esoteric to you, particularly if you've just started moderating. If you're an experienced moderator, you'll relate. I invite you to mark the ones you don't fully understand, as those will typically be the ones where you have room to grow. A code of conduct has consequences if not followed and great rewards if followed. Consequences will always be less-than-desired experiences by the member or member turnover, and rewards are referrals, high retention, and overall feelings of great satisfaction in running meetings.

Be Selfless

- Make no mistake: as the moderator, you're not better than the member. And it's the mentality that the moderator *is* better that leads to decisions that aren't best for the group.
- Don't reveal information about another member except as a teaching moment and never if it was privileged information. Being *in the know* about someone is really just a euphemism for gossip, and there's no place for that when you're moderating.

- Put the well-being of the council above your own. If you seek a victory for yourself, it will always be to the detriment of the council. You're victorious when the group is.
- You don't have all the answers. And even if you think you do, you shouldn't be sharing those answers, as you're not operating in a consultant capacity. Your wisdom is shared only after the council members have all shared their insights. Related is that you're not the center of attention.
- Your behavior ripples through the PaC, especially in the beginning. You're modeling acceptable behavior, and whatever you allow will be assumed allowable by members. If you raise your voice, the members will think that's OK and will raise their voices as well.
- Don't take sides; stay neutral. Even if you have a strong opinion, you exist to help the members identify and voice their own thoughts. The PaC meeting isn't a soapbox for the moderator.
- Meetings aren't rescheduled for your benefit—only for the benefit of the members.

Trust the Process

- Style is not a substitute for substance.
- Don't impose your own personal agenda or value system on the council, don't make assumptions, and if a member says something you don't approve of, that doesn't make what they said illegal or immoral, and it doesn't make them wrong.
- Don't fit the council's energy; be a force for raising it. Be uplifting.
- Shed light on and create awareness of what's happening.

- Silence is good. Silence is required for members to process, think, reflect, and get to the heart of the matter. Recognize that members process at different speeds. If some are quick to defend, they're probably not processing the information, not listening, and avoiding being open and absorbing the feedback.
- While you're technically the "leader," you'll actually follow.
- Don't force the process; force will cost you the support and trust of the members, and at times it will create conflict.
- Your PaC will evolve naturally. It's self-regulating and will work itself out.

   - If there's silence, let it grow; something will emerge.
   - If there's a storm, let it happen; it'll resolve into a calm.

Pay Attention

- Don't favor some behavior over others, or performance over others, or members over others.
- Observe and take note of all behavior; it tells a story and gives insight about the member.
- Be careful of the members who dominate and squelch the input of others or are always first to respond. Similarly, watch for members who aren't speaking.
- Keep everyone in the present and engaged.
- Know when to act, listen, and withdraw.
- A well-run group isn't a playground of egos. No one is right. Only the members can decide for themselves what's right for them.

- See things before they happen or as they unfold. For example, be on the lookout for members getting antsy and needing a break or a member getting emotional. The latter might prompt discussion or trigger the need to slow down or pause for the person to regain composure.
- Recognize potential mountains while they're tiny hills, such as a controversial comment made by a member that causes the other members to visibly react. Stop and ask the member to clarify and allow members to voice their thoughts. Don't let things fester.

Inspire Others

- Keep a culture of openness, integrity, and trust.
- The moderator doesn't outshine the council; instead they encourage the members to shine.
- Create time for reflection in the council meetings. The perfect times are right after processing a COPI, and at the end of the council meeting, asking members to reflect and identify a takeaway. *What was the one thing of value they received?*
- You can't make people do what you think they should do. And trying won't lead to their clarity or learning.
- Remember that you're helping others find their successes.
- Share your successes and experiences but not too much, and don't overshare. The focus is always on making the other members look good. Too much of your successes can cause you to be viewed as a member or the expert, which puts you into the Mastermind-group definition. Don't overshadow them.

Now that you have an understanding of what the role of a moderator really is, what is the experience like? What does the journey look like from new moderator to seasoned moderator? In the next chapter, I'll lay that out for you and guide you to delivering your best moderator self, resulting in an exquisite experience for your members, and a joyful, satisfying experience for you.

💡 Takeaways

- Skills of being are essential to developing into a great moderator.
- The ultimate meeting goal is to have many illumination moments.
- Illuminations come from Power Questions.
- Self-audit every meeting.

📇 Resources

- Download the Moderator Audit using the QR code at the back of the book.

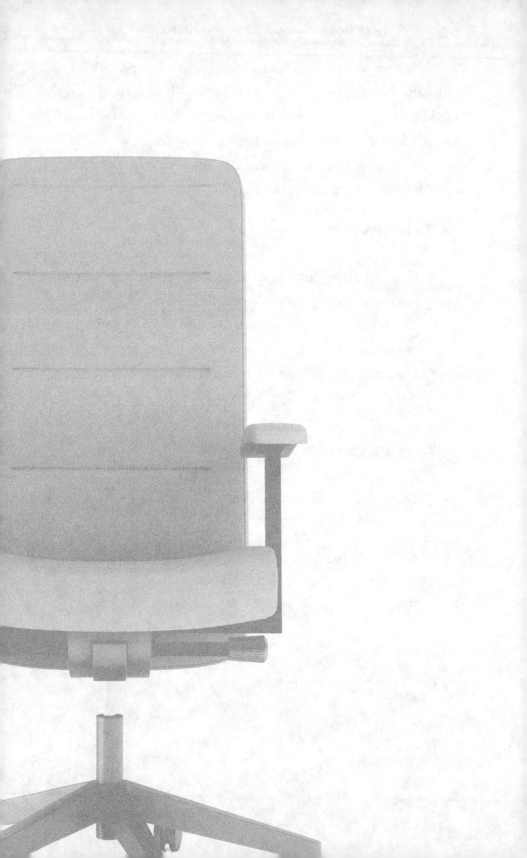

CHAPTER 7

The Moderator's Journey

Experienced, proficient moderators make running PaC meetings appear effortless, but the reality is far from it. So what was their journey like to get to this point of seeming effortlessness? What can you expect your journey to be like, whether you're just beginning or you've been moderating for some time? The Moderator Journey Map will illustrate that success is a journey, not a destination. The *doing* is often more important than the outcome, and this chapter will focus on that doing—that journey.

The Seven Stages of the Moderator's Journey

There are seven stages of a moderator's journey: stages 1 through 3 are related to launching your PaC business; stages 4 through 5 are learning and understanding the nuances of the meeting structure and moderating; and stages 6 through 7 address the advancement into being more strategic with your PaC. I'll discuss what to expect from each stage, including the most common challenges, such as things that reliably go wrong. Challenges can create a certain level of stress, and the key to managing that stress is to prepare for how you'll handle yourself when "things happen." It might not be fun to deal with these missteps, misunderstandings, and obstacles, but just knowing they'll likely happen will reduce your stress level and give you the confidence to maneuver to a successful outcome and into the next stage. Let's get started learning what you can expect during your tenure as a moderator.

Stage 1: Anticipation and Excitement

In the beginning, you're excited about your decision to become a moderator and lead a PaC. You anticipate and visualize yourself running groups, the members you'll have, and the income you'll generate. You're either building a business to create a legacy or creating a lifestyle for yourself. Neither is right or wrong, but you'll need to choose as the decisions that follow will be in the service of that decision. Do you want to build multiple groups and be able to pass the groups on to a new moderator or moderators (legacy)? Or do you plan to run your PaCs as long as you can, integrating them into your personal lifestyle, and someday winding down the groups?

Anticipation Excitement

MAKE A COMMITMENT

LEGACY OR LIFESTYLE DECISION

DECIDE YOUR CATEGORY OF PAC

ANNOUNCING YOUR NEW GIG

I think of this stage like the day you decide to buy your first car or a new car. Each time I transition to a new car, there's excitement and anticipation. I have to decide whether I'm keeping this car forever or whether it's a short-timer. When I decide on the type of car, I begin telling all my friends about it. I'm looking for validation—for support of my decision.

What to Expect

Opinions: Once you start telling friends and family about your decision, you'll discover who your supporters are. Be prepared for naysayers telling you it's a bad idea. Begin surrounding yourself with mentors, supporters, and experts who will help you on this journey.

Stage 2: Learning and Overwhelm

Now that you've made the decision to moderate your own PaC, it's time to get educated. Getting educated may mean talking to experts or others who are already moderating, taking a class or a course like our Peer Advisory Council Academy, or even what you're doing now—reading this book. A mistake many new moderators make is thinking they know it all. They jump right in and start putting a group together, and they quickly experience the consequences of their hastiness. There's inevitably some sort of unintended fallout for members because a decision was made that was good for the moderator but not for the group. The impact of the misstep is felt by the

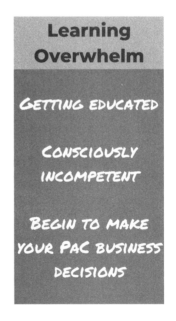

entire group. All manners of cleanup, backpedaling, and crisis control are necessary.

At the start of stage 2, you don't know what you don't know, and by the end, you know what you don't know. This is when a sense of being overwhelmed sets in because there's way more to know than you imagined. In chapter 9, you'll learn all the decisions you need to make before selling even one membership and how to avoid wreaking havoc on your group.

What to Expect

Procrastination. Most new moderators aren't aware of the myriad decisions they'll be faced with. If you're a slow decision-maker, the moment you notice all these decision points can be terrifying and lead to mental paralysis. If you're a fast decision-maker, be sure you think through the pros and cons of each decision. The key is not to procrastinate. Decide and move on; you can always change your decision.

> A mistake many new moderators make is thinking they know it all.

Not Prioritizing. Far too many new moderators get bogged down in planning to plan and take little to no action for weeks, months, or even years. There's a balance between planning and getting on with it. Be sure whatever you're doing is moving you forward and is the most important thing for you to do at that moment. At the same time, be sure you've allocated appropriate time to build your PaC. In the beginning, this isn't a part-time job. It's a full-time job that involves

- setting up the business,
- getting your materials branded,
- making the basic decisions (again, chapter 9),
- getting educated about your category,
- marketing,

- prospecting,
- networking,
- selling,
- putting the group together, and
- planning your first meeting.

If you can't devote two hundred hours over sixty to ninety days, you likely will not launch.

Stage 3: Awareness and Confirmation

In stage 3, you'll be laying the foundation for identifying members for your PaC. It'll feel good to hear positive confirmation from centers of influence (COIs), other acquaintances, and referral sources. These conversations help reshape any decisions you made that need adjusting due to new information you gathered. You'll try out your value proposition pitch (i.e., elevator pitch) and finalize any details about your category you were unsure of. You'll become aware of how much you know about your PaC category, including who your competition is and what you need to do to close any education gaps you have. These conversations will also help determine when to have a marketing event for

Awareness Confirmation

FINALIZE DECISIONS

PLAN FOR LAUNCHING

IDENTIFY PROSPECTS

TALK TO COIs, REFERRAL SOURCES, ETC.

prospects, or at a minimum, when to begin holding one-on-one Discovery Calls or meetings.

What to Expect

Practice, practice, practice. I don't know anyone who likes role-playing, but role-playing is an essential element for success. Role-play your messaging, and get your documents ready for membership, as well as any other sales tools you need to close new members (e.g., membership form, brochure, testimonials, sample agendas, etc.). Practice with family, friends, and close colleagues—anyone who will give you honest feedback.

No shortcuts. One thing I learned early on is that I could never do enough in the first stages of launching. If I thought I'd exhausted all angles to get referrals, there was always more I could do. I could always make one more attempt to reach someone. And any time I gave 1 percent more effort, it turned into a 10-plus-percent result. Every time I thought, "Oh, that's not that important to worry about or do," it was. You can't skip one step. For proper execution and implementation, every step is crucial and plays a role in the outcome.

Stage 4: Progress and Hope

When you're getting positive feedback, you feel like you're progressing. You have reason to think you'll actually launch a group. Progress is most felt in this stage because there are so many firsts: first marketing event, first networking event, first Discovery Call with a prospect, first member sold, and after many more members, your first group comes together. Before you know it, it's time to plan for the first meeting.

What to Expect

The first-meeting agenda is different and heavy on step 1. You may recall from chapter 5 that step 1 (The Opening) is for announcements,

MyTransition, and COPIs. However, the first meeting of a new group is different in that it's focused on introducing the members to each other and explaining the process for each part of the agenda. You'll also need to review the guidelines and secure member commitment to them. This meeting is about clarity and expectations, making sure that everyone is on the same page. For this first meeting, the more time you spend in step 1, the bigger payoff you'll see down the line.

Progress Hope

FIRST MARKETING EVENTS

FIRST PROSPECT DISCOVERY CALLS

FIRST MEMBERS SOLD

FIRST FORMATION OF YOUR GROUP

PLAN FIRST MEETING

Repetition. Early on, you'll underestimate the need to reiterate processes, expectations, and group guidelines. It's human nature to forget or not understand the first or second time you're exposed to something new. Repetition is necessary to build good habits in your members so you can take the group to another level. If they cannot master the MyTransition process, for example, they'll remain distracted, which means they're not showing up as good members to others. Remember that as a moderator, you lead by example, so one way to tackle this is to make sure your own transition into a meeting mentality is swift and well done.

Protect conflicts of interest. This means two things: conflicts of interest between members and conflicts of interest between members and you. Members can develop conflicts around how they think, or they might develop similar business ideas, which can cause conflict. You can also be in conflict when your business model is aligned with what's best for you instead of your members.

An example is having a termination clause of ninety days versus a shorter time frame. If a member wants to or has to leave the group, they're already out the door mentally. This is no different from an employee submitting their resignation letter. Rarely do you want an employee around for an extended time unless it's for training or transitioning a new employee into their role. But a member resignation is not an employee resignation. A member is a client. Holding them to paying you for ninety days more will only deteriorate the MX and create bad will in exchange for that ninety days of revenue. It doesn't help the existing group to know a member is leaving yet continuing to interact with them. If they know the member isn't continuing, they won't want to invest more time into them.

> For proper execution and implementation, every step is crucial and plays a role in the outcome.

Manage silent judging. Be prepared for new members and existing members to be judging everyone. They're all wondering what value others might have to offer them. It's common to have members observe and make judgments about who's a true peer or who's the smartest person in the room. It's your job to mitigate this mindset and set each member up to project their best so the other members can see why you believed they were a good fit for the group.

Stage 5: Uncomfortable and Optimistic

It's now time to actually run a meeting! You're feeling uncomfortable with running the meeting because you don't know what to expect, yet you're optimistic because you prepared and have a great group of members who are looking forward to this day. Being uncomfortable will last awhile. *Why?* Because it takes time to experience all the nuances. You can't read a textbook about them; you have to experience them and work through your discomfort.

What to Expect

Chaos. The most chaotic times are right before each monthly meeting and during the meeting. Chaos comes from not being able to anticipate how each member will show up for the meeting mentally, in addition to the unexpected or urgent challenges that don't reveal themselves until the moment everyone has arrived.

Uncomfortable Optimistic

FIRST MEETINGS

FIRST QAS OR 121

FIRST FALSE START

FIRST TURNOVER

FIRST MEMBER DRAMA

MEETING CADENCE BUMPY

YOU'RE BLIND-SIDED

FEELING LIKE YOU HAVE TO DELIVER MORE VALUE

Chaos takes on many forms, and some of them are unavoidable, despite your best efforts to be prepared. Here are some examples:

- A member's last-minute cancellation. Cancellations can have a major impact when that person was scheduled to present. This can leave you with a big hole in the agenda.

- The first false start, when the member you just sold is a no-show or has even changed their mind about joining.
- The countless last-minute texts from members who are running late or who forgot about the meeting despite your multiple reminders.
- Your first member drama, where the member suddenly breaks down emotionally because something bad happened in the business or in their personal life.
- The member who's always happy and supportive is suddenly silent and withdrawn.

What you can predict is uncertainty. Anticipating possible situations can eliminate many challenges from happening. Noticing behaviors that seem to be brewing and addressing festering issues quickly is always the way to prevent big issues from forming.

> **What you can predict is uncertainty.**

The need to stay silent. Members—not you—need to step in to fill the void. An example is when you have a member get emotional. Let the other members come to the rescue, not you. If your members are looking to you to take the lead, briefly do so, but step back so the other members can step in.

Taking the agenda for granted. It's easy to get into a rut with your agenda after many months of doing it because in one sense, it's the same four steps every meeting. But in reality it's much more, as what's under each step differs each month. Taking time to customize the detail under each step is what makes an exquisite MX.

Plan for a mishap. Think of what could go wrong, and plan for it. Be sure all members are reminded of the meeting location and time or video link, as well as actions they committed to via multiple channels of communication (e.g., text, call, email, calendar reminder). Make sure to use the form of preferred communication they told you about during Orientation. Have all contact info in your phone so you can connect with them if the meeting is about to start and they haven't arrived. Have a relevant backup agenda item in case you need to fill in time because of a cancellation. Think about what you'll do if food is late, technology doesn't work, or the weather is bad.

Members forget guidelines or you forget one. If you don't push for excellence and lead by example, neither will the members. Low expectations lead to members not taking accountability seriously, not showing up without letting you know in advance, etc. Many times, this is plainly due to members forgetting what they committed to. So it's time to remind them. You get the behavior you expect, so expect good behavior. You'll also have a moment when bad behavior is happening, and you realize you never discussed it. Be sure to discuss it at the next meeting. It's normal to have both of these happen repeatedly because members change and your group evolves, which requires new norms.

Always adapting and pivoting. Most times, the agenda as you wrote it never happens. As the meeting evolves, discussions occur that you cannot plan for. These discussions happen only when the members in the room open up and allow deeper thoughts and feelings to emerge. Don't force an agenda on the members just to follow it. As opportunities arise to have rich conversations and continue important dialogue, gauge what your members need and want. Either continue the discussion, or move on to what's next. Don't be so rigid that you're going through the motions rather than orchestrating the ebb and flow of the meeting. This suggestion is unsettling for people who like to know what's coming and lean heavily on agendas. But the group needs you to be flexible and will always appreciate your ability to adapt.

Bad behavior. *What's bad behavior?* A member being mean, disrespectful, or confrontational or raising their voice at another member. If this happens, the key is to stop it from escalating. Once you do that, determine whether the group needs to talk out what happened or talk through what's happening in a calmer way.

I had this happen in a group that had been together for almost ten years. Before the meeting started, there were hints of a conflict in a member's description of a chamber of commerce board meeting that had occurred earlier. The conflict was so personal that one member couldn't even enter the meeting room and was pacing outside. I could have mediated a discussion between the two members, but that's not ideal. My job is to moderate and to make sure the group's source of support is the group. So I asked the group to step in and speak in private with each disgruntled member until we could come back together and further debrief as a group. It worked.

Repeated COPIs or no COPIs. There will be a member who repeats the same COPI over and over because they never resolve it or make progress. This is a sign they either don't want to address it but would rather whine about it, or they aren't getting what they need and require more clarity from the group. Either way, don't let COPIs repeat themselves. When this happens, it's a red flag to address. Alternatively, there will be a member who never has a COPI, or it's so minor the other members' COPIs trump it in importance and severity. Track COPIs by member, by meeting, so you're aware when a member has gone months without processing one. Work with them in your QAS or a 121 call to formulate a COPI, or do their member spotlight or Perspective Report sooner rather than later. Those reports will create meaningful COPIs for the members naturally.

Bad member decisions. It's inevitable. You'll sign up a prospect that shouldn't become a member of your group. Either you know that but you do it anyway, or you don't know that because of a poorly conducted Discovery Call. Either way, it's a bad "hire." Just like it's virtually impossible for a manager to have a 100 percent success rate in hiring for their organization, it's equally hard for you to have a 100 percent success rate for choosing right-fit members for your PaC. When it happens, swiftly address it by either coaching them up to be a great member or coaching them out gracefully. Use the old adage "Hire slow, fire fast." The moment you realize you made a mistake is the moment to address the situation.

The urge to deliver more. After a few meetings, you'll question whether the members are getting enough value. You'll ask yourself what more you can do. Should you send articles between meetings, add more to the agenda, call members between meetings, or introduce a leadership book to be read? None of this is necessary. What's necessary is to trust the agenda as it is, with its four steps. Concentrate on being sure that each step is executed well and that you have a well-planned agenda. This is where the members get the most value, so be sure not to rob them of those steps by introducing something more into the agenda. There's a time for doing something more, and that's in stages 6 and 7. Not here, not yet.

Stage 6: Momentum

Momentum

MEMBERS' TENURE
SURPASSES A YEAR

GROUPS FULL OF
DIVERSITY

GROUP
OWNERSHIP

GROUP CULTURE
FORMED

DIFFICULT
CONVERSATIONS

YOU AND THE
MEMBERS ARE
HAVING REGULAR
AHA MOMENTS

You're entering the fun stage of getting into a cadence and moving into finessing your style and the MX. You've had many, if not all, of the unpleasant experiences and know they're not as bad as they seem in the moment. You've survived them, and if you faltered, you learned what to do next time.

What to Expect

Group melding. The group is gelling. They know each other well through their Perspective Reports, they've had moments of vulnerability while developing trust and compassion, and they've realized the value of the group guidelines. They genuinely like each other and have each other's back. They also value different perspectives and have learned how to ask great questions that reveal those perspectives. This part occurs because of the skillful way you assembled the group, with an intention of including diverse perspectives, and because of the way you've skillfully moderated them. They wouldn't have gotten to this point without your great moderating.

Group ownership. The group has progressed to owning their PaC experience. This is "their" group. They participate in discussions about the fit of new members, they mentor new members, they're eager to help a member in need, they innovate the group experience by suggesting topics for discussion or a retreat, and they consistently elevate their own growth.

Having to do the hard work. Don't punt the hard work of disciplinary conversations or confronting bad behavior because doing so takes effort and you think it won't happen again, or worse, that no one noticed. Trust me; everyone notices bad behavior. Addressing rudeness, tardiness, unprofessionalism, unkindness, etc. is crucial and should be done immediately, but it shouldn't be confrontational. It can certainly be done with the same kindness you expect members to display to each other. Remember that respect is a two-way street that includes the moderator, and that the longer you go without addressing bad behavior, the worse it will be for everyone.

> Remember that respect is a two-way street that includes the moderator, and that the longer you go without addressing bad behavior, the worse it will be for everyone.

You will have to have a come-to meeting. When your group has gotten lazy (e.g., showing up late, violating the group's guidelines, not coming with meaningful COPIs after you've tried in the previous stage to correct this), it's time to get them back on track. This predictably happens around the year-one mark. And it might recur every couple years. The longer the group is together, the less it happens.

Address your concern as a group COPI. Put it out there that there's a group concern you want to raise for discussion. It works!

Capitalizing on opportunities. Until now, you've been so preoccupied with the cadence of the meeting and how to handle the unexpected that your mind isn't open to the sound of opportunities. These are moments when you hear something profound, and it appears the group has missed it. When this occurs, either wait and have the member who said it restate it, or chime in immediately with "Wait—stop one minute. What did you hear Melanie just say?" This causes them to reflect and try to figure out the answer. There are also opportunities for a member to elaborate on a success or learning. The point is to listen for when it's time to pause and have everyone let the knowledge sink in. This is all part of illumination.

Stage 7: Confidence and Humility

The last stage is the most rewarding for moderators. You receive your highest ROI here: return on involvement and investment—both. You experience a high sense of satisfaction in seeing the progress of your members and how they've bonded as a group. Furthermore, your confidence level is high because you've experienced the ups and downs of running a group, and you know how to flatten out the hills of chaos. You can be strategic with your agenda and plan tactics to challenge the group to reach new levels of vulnerability and effectiveness. Your hard work is paying off, and you're having fun without a lot of heavy lifting. You're not bothered by hiccups with members, as you've planned for most of them and can quickly respond to the ones you haven't planned for.

What to Expect

Complacency. Taking your members—and the ease with which your PaC operates—for granted. This can easily happen when you are used to a certain level of chaos and discomfort, and then suddenly everything's going swimmingly, so you take a breather. But you can't. Your members won't always be there; they won't all love every meeting. After years of being a member, you might think they'll be there for life, especially if you've become close with them personally. Always remember they're paying you for an experience, a service, a result. They evaluate every meeting to determine whether their time was worth it. Make sure the answer is always yes. You know when you're becoming complacent when you get blindsided.

The urge to stick with the same routine. Don't fix what's not broken, right? Well, that doesn't really apply here. Changing up the meeting sometimes is necessary to keep members on their toes and to stimulate different thinking and energy. There are many ways to mix things up and freshen the energy:

Confidence
Humility

COMFORT
WITH THE
PROCESS

HEALTHY
GROUP
CULTURE

YOU'RE MORE
STRATEGIC +
PROACTIVE

STRATEGIC
PLAN /VISION
FOR THE
GROUP

- Change the agenda around.
- Hold the meeting in a different setting.

- Do an activity or have a retreat in place of the regular meeting.
- Tour a company everyone admires.
- Enhance your agenda by adding a new template, a new format, or a different speaker or by recommending a relevant book to read as a group.
- Bring innovation and best practices to your members. Ask them for feedback and what they'd like.

Above all, don't let the meetings get stale. When you sense the energy starting to wane, have some fun and breathe some new life into your PaC.

Constant learning. If *you* stop learning, you become less and less relevant to your group. This makes it harder to recruit as well as retain members. No one wants to be part of something that's outdated. Being a thought leader means being current, if not cutting edge. What you can contribute matters, and you want to have relevant, timely information to share with the group. You want to show them that you're getting outside your comfort zone to do this, and they should too. It's the only way we grow! And when we grow as individuals, our businesses grow.

You can play hooky. Know when to let up. Know when the group needs a reprieve after a tough conversation or tough year or a tough month. I remember one meeting when the members of my very-tenured group all came in, and it was chaos. They were like little kids who had eaten too much sugar or seniors on their last day of high school. It was very unusual—very different from the previous fifty-six meetings together. Something was awry. They needed to play hooky, so we played hooky that day. With their input, we did some fun bonding exercises, had an impromptu roundtable discussion, laughed a lot, and broke early for lunch together. It was one of the best meetings we ever had. Was I a bit fearful of doing this and of them thinking they were paying me money that day to play hooky? Yes, but I also knew the consequence of not doing it was an ineffective meeting. Putting a meeting agenda (round peg) into a unique group mindset (square hole) wasn't going to happen that day.

You'll have moments when the group needs you to put your foot on the gas pedal to get them out of a rut and meetings at which you need to put your foot on the brake to give everyone some space and time to reflect or have fun.

Creating a vision and strategic plan. The group and you are now ready to create the future of the group. Because they have ownership over the group (previous stage) and have repeatedly experienced the full value of being a member, they're open to and embrace creating a vision and a strategic plan for the group. We call this *leveling up* the group; it gives them a path to even greater value. This is the moment the group is part of the fabric of the member's business. It's a cornerstone to their own strategic plan. It's a necessity.

Visions are powerful tools for people to coalesce around an idea. They are no less powerful in a PaC setting to inspire commitment to one another.

—JOHN FOSTER, PATHFINDER GROUP; CERTIFIED
MODERATOR, TAMPA, FLORIDA

What Causes Burnout When Running a Group?

You might not think burnout can occur when running a PaC, but after doing anything for a bunch of years, burnout is always possible. The trick is to notice when its seeds are first sprouting. This goes back to EQ and the self-awareness I discussed in the previous chapter. The sooner you catch the feelings associated with brewing burnout, the better. The primary sign is exhaustion. It's normal to feel exhausted after running a meeting because your brain represents just 2 percent of your total body mass but uses 20 percent of your body's energy. You use a lot of brainpower running a PaC meeting: managing the meeting structure, noticing and attending to verbal and nonverbal cues and emotions, timing discussions, and constantly thinking on your feet.

Fortunately, you can actively prevent burnout, largely by doing the right thing up front and addressing any mishaps or miscommunications quickly. If it's already in the works, though, you can catch it in its earliest stage if you're aware of the signs.

Here are my top ten causes for burnout and how you can avoid them.

1. **Exhaustion.** During the meeting, you're at your peak at all times, which can be exhausting. That's why after a meeting you need to take time to relax, do a different activity, or reward yourself for a meeting well done. You need a break to decompress and reflect on what went well and what to do differently next time. If you don't take that break, your exhaustion will remain and become chronic, and that leads to burnout.

2. **You're not having fun.** You can't be all work and no play. Having fun with the members socially as a group helps with bonding of the members (and their moderator!). Enjoy lunch or a coffee with them one on one as well. Encourage laughter and banter in the meeting. They need to have as much or more fun than you do. Fun for them means making each other laugh, teasing each other, telling stories, and sometimes goofing off during a break.

3. **Being surprised.** No matter how attuned you are to each member, you'll still be surprised when members last-minute cancel a meeting with you, cancel attending their meeting

suddenly, are no-shows with no notice, etc. It can be stressful because you may have to suddenly adjust the agenda if it was a member's turn to present. Or you had an important discussion or speaker planned, and you don't want to start until everyone is there, but if you wait, it will throw off the timing of everything else on the agenda. If you are someone who doesn't react well to sudden change, this can be unsettling. To combat it, know that it will happen, take it in stride, and have a plan for when it occurs. Decide in advance that you'll just move ahead as is, and all will be fine. Because it really will be.

4. **Turnover.** Having a series of turnovers can be disappointing and disheartening. It will happen; don't take it personally. It's never pleasant to lose a customer, and it can trigger a lot of effort. There's effort in managing the transition of the leaving member out of the group, effort in managing the perception of the remaining members as one of their peers is leaving, and then effort in replacing the leaving member. One of my tenured Licensed Partners says if there's a resignation, it always happens right before a meeting, never after it. Talk about a distraction! Minimizing turnover helps prevent a bad chain reaction—having to secure existing members, having to manage the transition of the member leaving, and selling a new, right-fit prospect as fast as possible.

5. **No accountability.** If members aren't doing what they agreed to do and others aren't holding them accountable, the responsibility will fall on you. As a result, resentment can build, and exhaustion can set in quickly, as you're doing the heavy lifting of always being the one asking the follow-up questions. To handle this, step 1 is you modeling the behavior of holding

others accountable, and then step 2 is asking the members to do it themselves. Sometimes you have to come right out and say the words if they're not getting the message.

6. **No expectations.** If the group hasn't created guidelines (as suggested back in chapter 3) that include expectations of attendance, norms of behavior, and what deliverables to prepare, then the group has no path, and chaos ensues. Because guidelines are vital to how the meeting goes as well as how the members behave, if you haven't taken the necessary time and energy to create it with the group, your moderating is going to be challenging. As soon as you realize you're missing a guideline, build a discussion about it into the next agenda, and have the group create it.

7. **You're doing a lot of 121s.** The easiest way to overschedule your time and quickly get frazzled is to do a 121 meeting with each member every month. I promise there will be last-minute requests to change appointments, and the situation soon becomes inefficient and unmanageable. These meetings aren't necessary unless you're being paid to be an executive coach as well as moderator. And if so, you should be paid accordingly. Don't mix the two as a package for participating in a group. You won't get adequately compensated for your time and expertise.

8. **Members arrive late or leave early**. Allowing this behavior, unless warranted, is the most disruptive of a meeting. If you don't address it, you'll have to manage the meeting to be shorter, not end it properly, and be receptive to bringing members up to speed for what they missed. It also sends a signal to the other members that the behavior is OK. It's not fair to anyone. Managing a meeting that starts late or during

which a member leaves early requires more of your effort and, over time, depletes your moderating energy.

9. **Doing it all yourself without member help.** Members should help give referrals or testimonials so you can attract the best fit for the group. It's in their best interest to do that. If you're doing all the labor involved in prospecting and selling, and especially if you have excessive turnover, you'll feel like a hamster on a wheel. You'll also want to train your members to lead by example so you're not the only one who can step into the role of moderator. For example, ask a member to ask the group for status updates rather than you doing that. This also helps reinforce the idea that the accountability in the group is between the members as peers rather than you and the members.

10. **Doing it all yourself without administrative help.** Always ask yourself what the highest and best use of your time is, and remember to reserve your energy for your members and the meeting. Delegate the things that aren't your strengths or aren't a good use of your time, such as detailed work, scheduling, meeting logistics, etc. Doing things you're not great at or don't enjoy is depleting.

Succession: Can Another Person Run Your Peer Advisory Group?

Succession Transition

LIFESTYLE:

WIND DOWN

PART-TIME

LEGACY:

CONTRACTED MODERATOR

SELL OR KEEP AND OUTSOURCE

TRANSITION PLAN

The beauty of running your PaC is that you can transfer it and keep ownership or sell it. You have choices. But only if you set it up correctly. Another person can run your group if one rule is adhered to: *the focus is always on the group.* It has to be about them and not about you. It's not about them if you can answer the question better than they can or if you share your expertise prior to getting their thoughts. If it's about you, then no, another person cannot run your PaC.

You know it's not about you when your members are in stage 3 below. These stages are from the member's perspective when talking to someone about their participation in one of your PaCs. Note the shift in ownership.

Stage 1: "I am a member of [your name as the moderator]'s group." The peer group concept generically takes on an identity as a whole. Members aren't feeling connected to the group and still see it as yours.

Stage 2: "We are members of the same peer group." Members identify with the group they're in, and they include the other members.

Stage 3: The ultimate. "My peer group ..." Members identify the PaC as their own; they have direct ownership. The key word here is "my."

One of the key milestones to having a great group is when the members go through the member journey—from "a group," to "our group," to "my group!" The candor, the energy, and the care for each other are clearly elevated once the group gets there. That's when real transformation can happen.

—JORGE TITINGER, TITINGER CONSULTING; CERTIFIED
LICENSED PARTNER, GREATER NASHVILLE, TENNESSEE

The goal is to advance them as quickly as possible to stage 3, which creates retention, ownership of the experience, and a higher level of achievement.

How do you get the best replacement to run your specific group? The person has to be perceived as possibly more talented than you in business. Their talent should have synergies with you or be of a background complementary to the group. As long as they have one trait or skill set you don't have, the group will believe the transition is an upgrade. A best practice is to immediately showcase an area of their expertise so that there's no question they're beyond qualified.

I have transitioned nearly twenty groups, some multiple times between moderators, without losing a single member. How do you successfully ease yourself out and the new moderator in? I recommend doing it over ninety days or three meetings. The magic formula I've found is this:

- **Meeting 1:** The existing moderator runs 90 percent of the meeting, and the new moderator runs 10 percent of it. The new moderator's 10 percent showcases their personality. The objective is for the members to see potential in the new moderator. One-to-ones are held between this meeting and meeting 2 for the new moderator to meet each member, learn about their experience in the group, hear about their FORD, and share anything relevant from their background.
- **Meeting 2:** A fifty-fifty split between the existing and new moderator. The objective is for the existing moderator to begin taking a back seat and the new moderator to shine.
- **Meeting 3:** The new moderator runs 90 percent of the meeting and showcases their expertise with a short exercise or workshop; the existing moderator runs 10 percent (usually the most minor part of the agenda).

The existing and the new moderator share the moderation, and both participate in all aspects of the agenda. After the third meeting, the members are mentally transitioned to the new moderator, and you should be good to, literally, go!

What happens if you have to exit suddenly due to an illness or long-term emergency situation? Start preparing now by identifying someone who can take your place. It could be an existing member or a center of influence. But always have someone in mind. You don't want to be irresponsible, with no one to step in and your group floundering.

Members count on you to be the glue, and you owe it to them to be sure they can continue.

Now that you know what to expect in your journey as a moderator, how long will it take you to get to and master stage 7? I have no idea; it's different for everyone. What I will say is it'll take at least eighteen months and usually closer to four years. Stage 7 is infinite. It's always evolving, and just when you find one aspect is going well, another one needs adjusting. All of this is moving toward providing members with such an exquisite experience that they become satisfied members for life.

It's time to take a deeper dive into what it takes to retain groups and members for the long term.

🧠 Takeaways

- Moderating is a skill that takes time to perfect.
- No matter whether this is a hobby or a legacy, plan to transition the group one day.
- Stuff happens; it's part of the journey. Learn from it and move on. It will be OK.

Resources

- Download the Moderator Journey Map using the QR code at the back of the book.

CHAPTER 8

Retaining Groups and Members Long Term

———

Your ultimate goal as a PaC moderator is to create a level of satisfaction in your members that will transform them into lifelong clients. Your highest ROI will come when you minimize turnover and sustain engagement. This chapter will show you why and how.

Diving Into the Why of Member Retention

If a member is having a consistently good experience, they'll remain a member. Unless they sold their business, died, or moved, if they drop out of your PaC, it's because their member experience isn't providing them with adequate value. Let that sink in. Member retention, therefore, is the ability to keep a member satisfied for an extended period. Given that, you should never be surprised when a member leaves your

> **Never be surprised when a member leaves your PaC.**

PaC. If you are, you're out of touch; you're not paying attention. Because if you were, you'd see the red flags.

The importance of retention cannot be overstated, as it's technically most of your revenue. You have new members, and you have recurring revenue from existing members. That's as close to passive income as you're going to get, but it's not really passive as you have to earn it by continually providing French-Laundry-type experiences. Retaining members should be easier and less expensive than acquiring new members, plus they're like force multipliers in that they will refer friends and family and act as mentors for new members. Let's take an even closer look at the power of retention.

- **Affordability.** It's five to twenty-five times more expensive to acquire a new member than it is to retain an existing member.[8]
- **ROI.** A member-retention rate increase of just 5 percent can increase your company revenue by 25 to 95 percent.[9] And it saves you time, as you can spend less time prospecting to replace members and more time prospecting to grow your PaC. Furthermore, when someone leaves (we call this termination), there's processing involved, similar to the onboarding process for someone new. Again, time saved.

---

8   Amy Gallo, "The Value of Keeping the Right Customers," https://hbr.org/ (Harvard Business Review, November 5, 2014), https://hbr.org/2014/10/the-value-of-keeping-the-right-customers.

9   Ibid.

A Common Way to Calculate Member Retention Rate

OF MEMBERS AT END OF PERIOD –
OF MEMBERS ACQUIRED DURING PERIOD

$$\div$$

(# OF MEMBERS AT START OF PERIOD) X 100

For example: Imagine you start the year with twenty members, gain five new ones in the first quarter, and have one member leave. Here's the calculation of your member retention rate:

(24 – 5 / 20) x 100 = 95 percent retention

Or let's say you have forty-four members; you gain twelve, and thirteen leave.

(43 – 12) / 44) x 100 = 70 percent retention

To use this model yourself, remember to use the same period (e.g., annually or biannually) for all the variables. Once you know your rate, consider doing an audit of the members who left in search of patterns. For example: Why did they leave? Is there any similarity in the characteristics of members who leave? You might find that members in certain industries, at a specific stage of company maturity, or at a certain company size are more likely to leave than others. The audit can even reveal a blind spot, where you have a tendency to bring on a member but you shouldn't, as discussed in chapter 2. When I did my own audits, I found that in most cases, when a member left, I had skipped a part of the process. I didn't do a thorough interview (Discovery Call) or fit Orientation in after their first meeting. Both would have revealed missed red flags prior to starting. Usually members left because they weren't a true peer of the group in sophistication. Looking at the hard data will bring to light vividly what to do and not do going forward. It's a way to hold yourself accountable and learn from your mistakes.

Other benefits to high retention include the following:

- **Loyalty.** Retained members buy more often and spend more than newer members. They've gotten to know and trust you. Think of your consulting services here. Retained members are built-in consulting clients.

  ▫ Consulting, if you choose to do it, can mean an exponential increase in lifetime value of the member. When I had my franchise, there were two reasons why consulting increased the value of my business:

    1. All members who used my company for consulting engagements had higher retention rates. I knew their business better and could help them succeed faster by knowing what COPIs to bring to the group, plus I helped them implement the exceptional insights they received from the group. In other words, implementation equals results.

    2. Consulting gives you multiple revenue streams from the same client. This was one of the reasons my franchise sold for a higher multiple to a strategic buyer—the

Your cost of acquisition basically goes to zero with a referral.

combination of member recurring revenue and consulting revenue.

- **Referrals.** Satisfied, loyal members are more likely to sing your praises and refer their friends and family. This is like outsourcing your prospecting and not having to pay for it! Your cost of acquisition basically goes to zero with a referral. And it's the fastest way to organically grow.

- **Intra-PaC member experience.** This is a unique business. It's a business where your customers (i.e., members of your PaCs) impact each other and all your members know each other. An excellent new member adds to the group's experience. A wrong-fit new member takes away from the group. One misstep impacts not just you and that member alone like it does most other companies, but it also impacts all members of the group. Additionally, when one member leaves, the others silently evaluate their participation. If one was on the fence whether to continue or not, it can trigger them to leave while another member is leaving. This is a huge risk and why later in this chapter I discuss the importance of offboarding. One less member decreases the energy in the room, the diversity of opinion, and the wisdom in the room. When one member joins the group, the other members get validation of their membership. The reverse is true as well.

> One misstep impacts not just you and that member alone like it does most other companies, but it also impacts all members of the group.

The Discovery Call in the sales process is designed to uncover red flags for long-term retention. It won't uncover everything, though. Your best barometer is your observation of your members' actions and behavior and listening to what they say. Let's describe some of those red flags so that you can easily detect them.

The Red Flags

As I mentioned, it should never come as a surprise when someone wants to leave your PaC. There are always signs, and if you're paying attention, you'll notice them the moment they arise (and address them the moment they arise). Here are my top ten signs that a member is potentially considering termination and what you can do about them.

1. **They have cash flow problems.** *How do you know?* They allude to it in the meeting but don't want to process it as a challenge. Or their payment is regularly late, or their credit card is continuously declined for their membership dues.

   What to do: Encourage them to bring up cash flow or margins or money management as a COPI. If they don't want to, suggest talking to a member who's good with finances one on one. I've witnessed many members having cash flow problems, feeling they couldn't continue their membership. I always ask them to bring the issue to the group, even though they're usually embarrassed to do so. In many cases, as a result, their PaC finds significant opportunities to increase cash flow as well as kinks in the process causing cash flow crunches. Problem solved, and trust and connection deepened!

2. **They've missed two consecutive meetings.** And especially if the reasons are ones they can control. The meetings are a

priority. In my experience, if a member misses three meetings in a row, they've disconnected from the group, and the group has disconnected from them. Reentry into the meetings is difficult, as they've missed so much, and it usually falls on your shoulders to fill them in.

What to do: After the second meeting is missed, ask to move their 121 or QAS to as soon as possible. The key is to meet with them to discuss what's happening with their schedule that's causing them to miss meetings. Confirm they'll be in attendance for the next meeting, and bring them up to speed about what has happened in the last two meetings. Ask them to write a note to the group giving them an update on their own happenings with the business so the group sees their commitment and doesn't disconnect from the member. If it's a COPI that's causing them to miss meetings, plan to have it processed in the next meeting. And last, secure their commitment to making the meetings a priority, and support them in making that happen.

3. **They're not mentally engaged.** They look at their phone, they're late, they leave early, they don't have much to say, or they don't contribute anything of value.

What to do: Privately inquire about what's causing this behavior. Seek to understand, not condemn. You never know what's happening personally or professionally that's resulting in their distraction or disengagement. Your goal is to determine whether the distraction can be dealt with or removed or why they're not able to be present. Set some boundaries about technology use, and reinforce the guidelines you've set that the group agreed to. It's critical to catch this one early, as bad behavior by one member creates bad behavior by the other members. One member looks at their phone, and that triggers another member to look at their phone. And so on.

4. **They don't come with COPIs.** They haven't needed to process a COPI for over a quarter. They say everything is fine, but everyone knows it isn't.

    What to do: In your 121 or QAS, plan for the month they'll bring a COPI, and identify what it will be. You can also ask the group what COPI they think this member has that should be discussed. This is an advanced form of COPI identification, where other members tell a member they have a COPI. But when someone isn't engaged, this is exactly the type of response that triggers a shift in the member who is disengaged, as they realize the other members care about them, have been paying attention, and want to help.

5. **They're selling their company.** That means a new owner and it's unlikely they will fill the seat of your member because they're located elsewhere, not a fit, or not interested.

    What to do: This is the most important time for a member, as they can avail themselves of the group's wisdom. It's a defining moment for you as a moderator as well because how you handle this moment tells the group whether you're a true moderator and whether you trust the wisdom the group has to offer. This is a life-impacting decision for the member, and it needs to go well in your PaC. It's possible that part of the condition of the sale is the owner staying in the group through the transition to a new career or season in their life. Be sure to also ask for an introduction to the new owner to see whether they're a fit. When to ask will be case by case, as every sale transaction has its own timing and complications. Your member will know when it's the right time. When it is, it's especially effective to have the old owner at that meeting to reinforce the value.

6. **They're transitioning to a new leader.** This is more common in professional services firms where they rotate leadership. The new leader may not value the PaC membership and decline to continue or their personality might not be a fit for the group.

   What to do: Similar to the previous red flag, ask for an introduction to the new leader to determine whether they're a fit.

7. **They miss your QASs or monthly 121s.** This indicates they're not prioritizing planning time with you or they don't value it. You have to determine how much of the issue is you and how much is them.

   What to do: Be persistent about scheduling a meeting as soon as possible so you can discuss what's happening. If it's possible to do this in person, that's best. Maybe even do it over breakfast or lunch if you can. Everyone needs to eat!

8. **They're noticeably stressed or having trouble keeping commitments.** They don't follow through on calling you

back, don't fulfill their commitments from the previous meeting, and always have excuses.

What to do: One tactic is to meet the issue straight on during the meeting when everyone is giving updates on commitments. Ask the member what's happening and why they're missing the commitments they made. Are the commitments not meaningful enough or too big to tackle, or are they not good at implementing? Bring the issue out into the open, and ask the members for their observations as well. Be sure to ask the member what support they might need.

9. **They're having or anticipating a major life event or crisis** (e.g., death in the family, illness, divorce) that will distract them from commitments.

   What to do: Support, support, support. Be there, be a Resource Connector, and have the members take turns checking in on them to show compassion.

10. **They don't take the advice of the group, or you don't see progress** (and neither of you can articulate the value they're receiving).

    What to do: Be careful not to sign a member who's a *joiner*. Joiners join groups just for the sake of belonging to them and without the intention to change or work on themselves. Change is uncomfortable, scary, and unpredictable, and they don't like it. They would rather stay in the known instead of venture into the unknown. It's also possible that where they are isn't painful enough, or they're otherwise not motivated enough to change. When it's time for an update on progress and there is none, stop and dive into why. Moderate and create space for the other members to step in to help.

I'm sure you noticed that the common thread in what to do is address the situation immediately. Above all, you want the member to feel supported and cared for, and you want them to feel the benefit of being in your PaC. Whatever their issue is, they have a group of people who are there for them and will help them through it. *That's* how you bring a member back from the brink of termination.

I have found that it is always better to address a sign that a member may be questioning whether or not to stay in the group before the member comes to you with it. This is best done by talking (not texting or emailing) to the member and getting a feel for what is happening with them.

—BRAD SEAMON, SEAMON COACHING AND CONSULTING;
CERTIFIED MODERATOR, BALTIMORE

The Importance of Being Proactive

Although there's plenty you can do once you've seen a red flag, it's preferable to be proactive and prevent the red flags in the first place. Here's what I recommend in general:

- **Focus on the COPI.** From the very start—onboarding, where you and your new member identify which of their COPIs is most important—you have the opportunity to show a member how valuable your PaC *already is* for them. Processing that first COPI, no matter what it is, provides clarity for them, and clarity is value. Once some clarity is established, the odds of *aha* moments occurring rise.

▫ Another benefit of processing that first COPI is bonding with their peers, which is critical for retention because if a new member doesn't connect with them first, it's very difficult for your PaC members to connect with them. Existing members are naturally skeptical of new people if they don't see them raising real issues and being able to be open and vulnerable. Without a genuine connection, members don't take the meetings seriously, they don't prepare, they might be late, and they might not show up at all. They need to sincerely believe that this group of people is "their" people. When they do, trust is the result. With trust present in a PaC, its members don't hold back for fear of being judged, and they don't judge others.

▫ A new member is not fully onboarded until they go through the entire experience of being a member. That means processing a COPI, doing their Perspective Report or member spotlight, and having a Quarterly Achievement Session or 121 with you. This is why the first three months are so critical. It will take at least three months for them to understand and have the full experience of membership (MX).

> **A new member is not fully onboarded until they go through the entire experience of being a member.**

MEMBER
FULLY
ONBOARDED

- ☑ ORIENTATION
- ☑ PROCESS COPI
- ☑ PERSPECTIVE REPORT
- ☑ QAS

- **Share.** When members share personal as well as professional information, they connect better. Personal information opens the door to seeing others as more like us. As soon as you find out someone is from your hometown or has the type of dog you have or a teenage son and you do, too, you tend to like them more.[10] At the very least, there will be similarities on the business side, as that's why those members are all in the same PaC together.

- **Have socials.** In addition to meetings, whether spontaneous or planned, socials are an opportunity to be less structured and allow connections to arise. Socials can be a fun activity like bowling, shuffleboard, a baseball game, or a holiday happy hour. The intention is to see a different side of each other in a different environment. It can also be a chance to

---

10   Adam Hampton, Amanda Fisher Boyd, and Susan Sprecher, "You're like Me and I like You: Mediators of the Similarity–Liking Link Assessed before and after a Getting-Acquainted Social Interaction," https://journals. sagepub.com/ (Sage Journals, July 30, 2018), https://journals.sagepub.com/doi/abs/10.1177/0265407518790 411?casa_token=wWYItVusLHIAAAAA%3Ap_605aJW3wDT2zhhm7s8SgDnfz021uMOGt5j6B-r4PNAgnQtIht4wj sAK_CZHXXHkIcI80UYrAltvQ&.

meet spouses, significant others, business partners, or senior leaders who allow you to see a different side of your member.

> ◻ One tradition I did in my early days was an annual Member Appreciation event. I brought all members and their guests together to celebrate member successes, hand out member awards, and show my appreciation for their membership. Maybe that's a tradition you'd like to start!

- **Celebrate successes.** Whether or not you include this in your agenda, each meeting should involve some kind of celebration. This fosters appreciation and highlights expertise and accomplishment. It solidifies that the group is composed of smart people, and it creates admiration. Also, members rarely celebrate their own successes. Either they don't take time to do so or think it's not necessary. But it is. They can learn as much from their successes as they can from their failures, and this is a great opportunity for them to reflect and articulate what they've learned. It's also a silent reminder of accountability.

- **Communication.** Encourage regular member communication between meetings. This can be informal or formal, by assigning buddies (or asking them all to pair up) who agree to meet for coffee. You also want to regularly check in on each member yourself. Always call after the first meeting to see whether the meeting met their expectations, and then after the third meeting in your QAS or 121 meeting. You want feedback about how *you* are doing as a moderator and see how they are doing as a new member.

A Member Says They're Leaving. *What Now?*

When this happens, don't immediately panic. Above all, remain calm. This is an opportunity to connect with the member and to do so immediately. You have one objective—to understand why they want to leave and to change their mind, assuming you want them to stay. I have a termination policy that requires a mandatory thirty-day notice and is stated on my member contract, but the last thing you want to do is lead with the fact that they signed a contract and are required to stay another thirty days.

Have an open, curious, nonjudgmental attitude during this conversation. As I previously discussed, you shouldn't be surprised by an intention to terminate; there are almost always signs. But sometimes there aren't. Sometimes something has just happened in their business or family or with their financial situation, and they didn't see it coming or couldn't predict it, or it was a sudden event. In other words, there are circumstances that could warrant a temporary reduction in monthly dues or even a leave of absence from the group (e.g., travel or a situation that needs their full-time attention). The latter isn't optimal, but might be unavoidable. The former is preferable because your priority is to see if you can meet the needs of everyone—the member, by allowing them to continue as part of the group and keeping them engaged, and the group, because you avoid the disruption that comes with termination and leave of absence (although those feel different to everyone). Members who are permitted a leave of absence (LOA) are always grateful for that and find value in the flexibility. If a member really is going to terminate, they should come to their final meeting to thank the group, explain why they're leaving, and acknowledge the value they've received. You should also coach them to state that they recognize and will adhere to confidentiality even after leaving.

The First Three Months Are Crucial

A member's initial three months are the time they're most in jeopardy of leaving. This entire time, they're assessing the value they're getting for their time commitment. They're also figuring out whether the group is "their" people. It makes sense, then, that the more bonded they are with the group, the less likely they are to terminate. Notice I said bonded with the *group*, not you. It's essential that your goal is to get the member transitioned from the closest relationship they initially have—you—to having the deepest relationship with the members of their group.

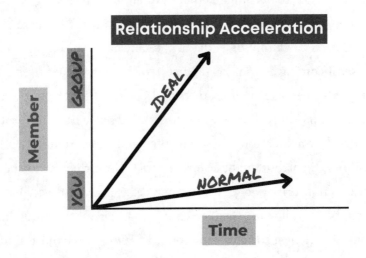

There are ways to nudge members to connect with the new person, and vice versa. Here's what I recommend for the first three months:

- Pair an existing member with the new member for mentoring *about being a member*, not mentoring in business. If they were referred by a member, consider pairing them with a different member so they develop another close relationship beyond the member they already know. Suggest they schedule a coffee meeting.

- Be sure the new member gets their COPI processed in meeting 1 or 2, at the latest. Sometimes new members want to observe more in their first meeting and will be more open to present their COPI in meeting 2 after observing the format.

  □ Make sure the new member presents their Perspective Report after observing an existing member presenting theirs. If you can, schedule the new member's presentation in month 4. That gives you time in your QAS or 121 in month 3 to help them plan for their report. It also gives them a sense of more value to come, motivating them to remain a member.

  □ As mentioned previously, seat the new member in the middle of the group so they feel included and not "on the outside."

  □ Be sure the new member doesn't have any housekeeping questions (e.g., billing, meeting attire, food allergies you might not know about impacting the food order, or general meeting questions). Resolving those issues takes that weight off their mind and helps them feel more comfortable sooner.

What Happens after Month 3?

A better practice is to have a plan for after month 3. Don't have a mindset that if someone gets to month 4, they're good to go. Month 3 isn't a hump to get over with a guarantee that they're settled into the cadence of meetings. Remember, a member isn't fully onboarded until they've experienced every aspect of their membership. In creating your ultimate MX, having a twelve-month plan for each member is smart business. I've found that in month 11, for example, members tend to go through a second reevaluation of membership. Intuitively, they know a year of participation is approaching, and they think about whether their PaC is worth the investment for another year. One way I've overcome this obstacle and made it easy to move into perpetual membership is to have plenty of value each month in addition to the meetings, such as the following:

- Finding articles related to their industry, goals, or initiative
- Creating member case studies
- Giving tips on how to take advantage of their membership
- Finding assessments or other tools they might benefit from
- Arranging a lunch or coffee date together or with another member
- Making a point to connect them with someone of interest or who can help them
- Sending a book or company-logo notebook for their use
- Connecting on LinkedIn and sharing or commenting on their posts or company posts
- Inviting them to an activity (e.g., attending an event with you, golf, networking meeting, etc.)

Strategies for Retaining Your Entire Group

In addition to being sure each member is retained, there's another layer of retention—making sure the group doesn't fall apart. Both individual satisfaction and group cohesion and satisfaction are required for PaC success.

Retaining each member does not equate to retaining the group. *Why not?* Because the member has to also be happy with the progress of the group. Is the group evolving and getting better together? Are the meetings being run well, or are they getting stagnant? Are you at the top of your game each meeting? Here are three strategies to keep your group progressing.

> **Retaining each member does not equate to retaining the group.**

1. **Do a strategic plan (strat plan).** Just like you do a strategic plan for your company, you should do one for each of your PaCs. This is a phenomenal exercise that each of our Licensed Partners do annually. It includes a SWOT on the group; a look at the metrics of attendance, COPIs per member, termination reasons, and membership-dues average; and a plan for what the group needs in the following twelve months regarding topics of discussion, new members, a retreat, speakers, etc. It's a game changer because it forces you to approach your PaC like a business. It reminds you that you need to be strategic with your actions and create intentional experiences. You can't just wing it from month to month and assume the group will be healthy, sustainable, and profitable for years to come. There's no such thing as putting your PaC on autopilot.

2. **Create a vision for the group.** In chapter 7, I introduced the idea of creating a vision for the group. A vision gives your group a forward-looking view into what the group could mean for them individually and together. This is no different

from a business leader having a vision for their company and communicating it to their employees. When there's a vision that everyone buys into, it creates energy and desire to achieve it. And retention!

3. **Remember the six attributes of high-functioning PaCs** I introduced in chapter 4. When you've chosen running PaCs as a business, you're in a similar position to a coach on a sports team or a manager developing their team. So think of your group as your team, and your job is to moderate to create that high-performing team. When you see that any of these attributes is low or missing, moderate to uplift it!

   a. They have respect for diversity of opinion and perspective.
   b. They have a commitment to continuous learning.
   c. They stand with other members.
   d. They are accountable.
   e. They have abundance thinking.
   f. They know how to be vulnerable.

In the final chapter, you will tackle all the decisions required to run an effective, profitable PaC.

💡 Takeaways

- Retention makes you money, and attrition loses you money.
- Address red flags immediately.
- Your members impact the experience of one another as well as you.
- Referrals are your lowest cost of acquisition.

- Treat your group like a business—have a vision and a strategic plan.

Resources

- Download a PaC Strat Plan Template by scanning the QR code at the end of the book.

CHAPTER 9

Before You Sell Even
One Membership

———

There are scores of questions and options to consider when deciding what's right for you *before* starting your PaC. Just like in a PaC meeting, in this final chapter, you'll learn how others make the decisions, and you'll figure out what's best for you. Your answers will give you direction and clarity on your path forward.

"Begin with the end in mind" is the second of the seven habits of highly effective people Dr. Stephen R. Covey defines in his bestselling book, *The 7 Habits of Highly Effective People.* It refers to starting with a clear understanding of your destination. At the most basic level, think about traveling. There you are, with your map or your travel app. How do you know which direction to go when you pull out of your driveway if you don't have an ultimate destination? You can't effectively, efficiently, drive one block if you don't know where you're going. The strategic planning you do before accepting one member into your PaC helps you identify your destination, and once you've done that, your path becomes clear.

"I get that, but I'm pretty sure I know what I'm doing and where I'm going."

At the risk of sounding dramatic, that's a dangerous statement. And what happens next is usually a combination of the moderator looking bad and the MX not going well. The reality is that you need to make all important decisions up front, and you might not even know what all of them are right now if you don't have experience running these groups as a moderator. No decision is still a decision, as it has consequences. One of those consequences is you revealing yourself as someone who hasn't thought about the issue and who needs to get back to the person with the question. Another one of those consequences is you making a decision on the fly, and few of us make good decisions that way. Another downside is that if you start to grow quickly and struggle to implement a solid program, proactive support for existing members can slip through the cracks. Handling situations on the fly that could have been predicted keeps you in tactical mode. Once you launch your first group, you want to be in strategic mode. Strategic mode keeps you ahead of the needs of your clients, not behind them. You wouldn't expect the French Laundry to figure out their menu after seating you for lunch, would you?

You have a lot of decisions to make before starting your peer group business. The following list is in priority order, and I suggest you use it that way. Each decision you make informs the next one specifically and all future ones as well. After each decision are questions to ask yourself as well as better practices I've learned from my own experience and from my Licensed Partners. Use our wisdom and approach this chapter with a beginner's mind. Don't assume you know all the answers or where I'm going with the questions; just try to be present with the suggestions.

A caution before you begin: This is an intensely personal decision. This is about *you*—what you know, what gives you energy, and what kinds of people you will be able to best serve. Don't try to replicate someone else's success. What they're doing works for them because of who they are! Now let's find out what will work best for you.

Category of Peer Group

Remember the types of PaCs back in chapter 2? Start there. It's possibly the hardest decision to get clarity on, and it sets the stage for other decisions, such as pricing, frequency, and delivery method. You don't want to end up like Jim, referenced earlier, who failed with his first group.

Here is a refresher on the six categories of PaCs:

1. Position, title, level of responsibility
2. Industry specific
3. Geography
4. Specialty (e.g., Family Firms, women-only, faith based, etc.)
5. Client community
6. In-company

Remember that there are two other parts to this decision, as the categories are necessary, but general. You need to get a bit more specific …

Three levels:

1. Entrepreneurial
2. Growth
3. Strategic

Three delivery methods:

1. In person
2. Virtual
3. Hybrid

Questions to Ask Yourself

What's your passion? Whom do you enjoy working with? Where's your expertise? What lifestyle do you desire? What PaC category resonates most with what level and what delivery method for you?

Better Practice

The better practice is whatever is unique to you. It's your personal decision on the type of group, level, and method of delivery. Just be sure you have a target audience large enough to put a group together. Too narrow a focus may make that difficult due to market size, limited connections, and Strategic Partner focus. Your idea should have built-in Strategic Partners you have access to.

Frequency of Meetings

How often you expect to have meetings with your category of peer group will dictate your pricing and parts of your agenda.

Questions to Ask Yourself

Do you want to do monthly meetings? Multiple times a month? Your delivery model will be important here. Do you want to take off certain months of the year, such as a summer month or a holiday week or month, because you suspect your members will value or even expect that? Will you have a retreat?

Better Practice

If you've chosen to meet in person and your group is for leaders, keep it at a monthly, four-hour meeting because most leaders can't and don't want to be in a meeting longer than that. It's difficult for them to remain present, and there's a diminishing return on their ability to focus for over four hours. However, there are many groups that meet for a full day. The key, if you choose to meet for a full day, is to have members who are able to be more strategic than tactical because they can tolerate longer meetings.

If you've chosen to meet virtually, usually a two-to-three-hour meeting is ideal once or twice a month. Virtual meetings take more out of you and are more prone to distractions. You can break up a four-hour format into two two-hour sessions or start with a three-hour format that makes the agenda tight but doable, as mentioned in chapter 3.

If you've chosen a hybrid model, finding the right combination of virtual and in-person-meeting lengths depends on the category of peer group you're moderating. You may want to incorporate a retreat day, a few meetings a year virtually sandwiched between in-person or full-day meetings if they are quarterly, based on members traveling. We have a Licensed Partner who does two months consecutively, virtually, with two two-hour meetings during those months, and then the third month is an in-person, four-hour meeting. The members love this because they work in a high-traffic, congested metropolitan area, and having two months of not battling traffic is ideal. Reconnecting in person quarterly keeps the connections strong.

Coaching or Quarterly Achievement Sessions?

I encourage those of you who have 121 coaching ingrained in your psyche to begin to charge separately for members who want coaching. Coaching is its own profession and service. In addition, you should transition to a Quarterly Planning Session (QAS), where you're meeting the member to review the last ninety days and the future ninety days of their participation in the group. And if you have a retention problem, analyze the coaching you're doing to determine whether it's contributing to the problem. Intuitively, you think it shouldn't, but ask your members whether they would prefer to continue a 121, coaching, or transition to a QAS. All three have different objectives and outcomes, as stated in chapter 5.

Questions to Ask Yourself

Are you a coach and want to incorporate peer groups into your coaching practice? If so, then charge appropriately to account for the proper value of each. How many groups do you want to moderate? If more than four, you can't do coaching, too, as there isn't enough time unless you are superhuman. Are you trained or certified to coach? If not, and you really want to do coaching, get certified. If not, don't do it. Would your target audience and members prefer 121s, coaching, or QASs?

Better Practice

The QAS maximizes your time and keeps the focus on the group, not you. Coaching risks the member relying on your 121s for answers rather than going to their PaC. Be sure to direct them back to the group if your coaching session turns into a consulting session. If it's really coaching, then your role is that of a coach, not someone with the answers. If you're providing answers, you should be paid accordingly for your consulting. Don't confuse the two.

Pricing

Pricing is a balancing act. You don't want to overprice and miss membership opportunities or underprice and not get paid what you're worth. And pricing must also match the length of meetings and whether or not you're doing coaching. Pricing is also under the definition of membership dues. It's recurring unless proper notice is given. So how do you figure it out?

Questions to Ask Yourself

What do the competitors charge? (Be sure it's an apples-to-apples comparison.) What will my market bear based on other services? What should my ideal member be able to afford? Am I doing coaching as a one-off or as an offering? (Again, this is not recommended unless you have a coaching practice and it's part of your strategy.)

Better Practices

Start with a fee you're comfortable with and feel you can justify. Then, with each new member opportunity, raise the price a little until you feel you've hit a ceiling. It doesn't matter that your members are all paying different prices. Trust me; they don't talk about what they're paying you, and if they did, you can justify it by when someone became a member. First in, lower dues. I've never had any member question me about their rate in comparison to someone else's.

Frequency of Membership Dues

When and how often will you charge for your dues?

 Questions to Ask Yourself

How frequent will you charge your members? Monthly, quarterly, annually? When during the cycle will you charge? Is everyone charged at the same time?

 Better Practices

Unless you have hundreds of members, charging at the same time is simpler and more efficient. Monthly recurring charges are less complicated and less noticed by the member. They are also easier to get from a prospect who's reluctant to pay annually without knowing for sure what the value is for them.

You may find tenured members who want to pay annually for tax reasons. And if you do take annual payments, be sure to manage your finances for the year accordingly. Annual payments give you peace of mind about the member staying. As for the member, the large, annual charge creates a decision in the member's mind of whether to renew or not when the annual payment comes due. If a member leaves earlier for some reason, you should never give a refund. If you choose to do so, you have to accrue these payments. I never wanted to manage that complexity and made it clear that there were no refunds *because I gave a discount for annual payments*.

> **Charge the month prior to the month of membership.**

Charge the month prior to the month of membership. For example, charge in May for June's membership. This way, you have no bad debt because you're getting paid in advance of providing services. And this allows time to resolve credit card declines before the member's meeting. I never had bad debt because of this. No member wants to be told they can't attend a meeting because they owe you money for it. I never had to do that because I believe they knew they were going to see me at the meeting and didn't want a declined card hanging over their head.

Length of Commitment

The length of commitment should match your pricing, meaning that how long you expect your member to commit to participating should match the amount of dues you collect. The reason is that you don't want to refund money if you can avoid it. There are a variety of situations to consider.

- Most new members won't initially commit for a long term. They need to be in the group for a few months first. So you can consider offering month-to-month billing for the first few months and then transition to annual.
- You can also give them an out for the first few months and then lock them into their annual commitment.
- Another option is to set an expectation that the members give the group at least three to six months before making a decision to leave. So they make a minimum commitment in the beginning, and then transition to your termination commitment (the length of time they have to give you notice).

Questions to Ask Yourself

How long do I want to ensure members stay committed to the group? What's reasonable for me to expect from the type of member I've chosen? What type of commitment will enhance the MX? What unintended consequences will occur with the commitment I choose?

Better Practices

Get a commitment for new members to stay a minimum of three to six months. The objective is to be sure they've been fully onboarded, and that takes three to six months. By then, they'll have experienced the full value of membership. You don't want an exit by a member who hastily made an uninformed decision. I found annual versus month-to-month commitment wasn't a decisive factor, as when a member wants to leave, they leave. And if they leave before their commitment is up, what will you do anyway? It's unlikely you'll sue them, and you don't want a disgruntled member in your meetings, feeling like they were forced to be there. Also, things can change so quickly and unpredictably. Members get sick, businesses sell quickly, etc. And if those situations arise, a member can't be expected to stay.

How to Charge for Dues

There are a variety of methods for collecting your membership dues.

Questions to Ask Yourself

What method will be convenient for you? Do you have capabilities set up for credit card or electronic funds transfer (EFT) transactions? Who will do the invoicing for you? Who will follow up with the members, answering their questions, resolving disputes, and addressing bad checks or declined cards?

Better Practices

Don't take checks. I can't stress this enough. You'll spend countless hours chasing why payment is late, and you'll be subjected to hearing "the check is in the mail" as well as reading it in emails. Checks are the road to bad debt and frustration.

The best practice is EFT payments, and credit cards are second but not processed by you. Get a bookkeeper or your accountant to process them. That way, they're the bad guy when you have to follow up with past-due payments. Electronic funds transfers are automatic and don't have processing fees. And you don't have lost cards or expiration dates to contend with as you do with credit cards. Consider giving a one-time discount for EFT processing; it will save you time and money.

Termination Clauses

You'll need to decide how much time you'll require your member to give notice. The purpose of the notice is for you to prepare the member to leave the group professionally, have time to replace their seat at the table, and have minimal disruption of the group and of revenue.

 Questions to Ask Yourself

What notice period is reasonable for my ideal member? How much notice do I actually need? How much notice would the group like to have?

 Better Practices

I've tested termination clauses of thirty days, ninety days, and annually. Intuitively, you might think the longer the better. But I had more

223

issues with the longer termination clauses. *Why?* Because there was always an exception as to why someone was leaving, and when the member has to leave, they have to leave. I can't and don't want a member to stay in their group uncommitted. It actually becomes contentious, and my objective has always been to have a leaving member leave with as good an experience as they got when they joined. The last impression is the last impression.

Thirty days' notice is my recommendation. *Why?* I expect them to come to one more meeting to exit properly. And it gives me a chance to replace them. While that's hard to do quickly, ideally I have someone in the wings to step in. And I don't want a not-present member in a meeting about to leave yet sitting there because they paid for it. That's a disaster. You want a member to exit well and move on quickly, replacing them so the group doesn't feel a void.

To Discount or Not to Discount

Sometimes it's appropriate to offer a standard discount or a one-time discount. Reasons might include getting a prospect to commit to membership or rewarding good behavior.

 Questions to Ask Yourself

Do I want to offer a discount for EFT transactions (reward for what's good for you)? What about a discount if someone wants to pay quarterly or annually versus monthly (reward for you and projected cash flow)? Do I offer a discount for founding members of a group (to get a group started sooner than later)? Would a discount be applicable to get an ideal prospect to sign and start their membership earlier than they wanted?

Better Practices

Discount only when there's a benefit to you as well. I'm not talking about a subjective benefit but a tangible one you can articulate to the member. In other words, only give a discount when you can say what's in it for them and what's in it for you. And any discount you give should translate into more dollars for you in the end. Otherwise, it's not good for business.

Be very careful about how much you discount because that discount represents hard dollars out of your pocket that you can't get back. For example, I have a Licensed Partner who decided to offer the first three months free for the founding members of a group. His philosophy was to provide a sense of urgency for them to sign up and stay committed for three months while he built the group to a full group. As a result, he has two groups of eight starting right away. Forfeiting three months of dues is expensive but not if it would take you two to three months to get the group going. Caveat: He has made sure the founding members have signed on to be fully paying members as of month four, and he has collected his one-time member fee (creating a financial commitment).

> *By offering the first three months as complimentary and only collecting an onboarding fee, I was able to launch two groups within ninety days.*

> —BOB PARENT, CATALYST GROUP, CERTIFIED
> LICENSED PARTNER, WINSTON-SALEM

Rate Increases

A commonly overlooked practice is the increasing of the standard rate for member dues. Part of the reason is that if you're using the methodology of market-based pricing, your new members are basically at market rate. That logic is only good until it's not, and you have neglected to raise the rate. It's human nature to not want to raise prices out of fear of losing members or having to have an uncomfortable conversation about value. And who likes to justify a price increase? So what happens is you don't, and it doesn't happen. Then, suddenly, your most-tenured members' dues are severely below market, and it's almost impossible to get that corrected. This oversight represents a lot of lost revenue for you!

 ## Questions to Ask Yourself

How frequently do you think you can do increases? When would you do an increase? How soon would you do an increase with a new member? What is your philosophy about price increases? When is it justified in your opinion?

 ## Better Practices

I suggest a quarterly increase of 1 percent, and it's stated in the membership application that they sign. This means I never—repeat, *never*—have to write an email justifying the increase. In addition, I never have to worry about someone leaving because I raised the price. It's automatic, it's fair, and it's out of mind for both the member and me once the application is signed.

One-Time Fee

Charging a one-time fee along with membership dues is common and essential. It's essential because it pays for your time to onboard a new member, the time and effort you spent to make the sale (i.e., the cost of acquisition), and any hard expenses for their membership. Hard expenses could be member binders, materials, or books, as well as your tools for onboarding, such as assessments and any proprietary intellectual property you've developed that they'll have access to. The one-time fee ensures you get a financial return immediately, regardless of whether the member ever makes it to one meeting. Yes, sometimes there's attrition between the time you onboard and the first meeting. Stuff happens through no fault of anyone!

Questions to Ask Yourself

What will be included in my onboarding to increase my MX? What has hard costs and soft costs associated with it? What's the perceived value of each? What margin do I need to make or want to make?

Better Practices

A rule of thumb is to charge at least the equivalent of one month's worth of dues and no less. This may not be enough if you have a lot of value-add packed into your member offering in addition to the monthly meeting. What's important is that you can justify the value and that it's a selling point for the membership, while enhancing and directly improving the member's experience.

PS: Be stubborn about never waiving this fee because it'll be your highest-margin revenue benefit. It always made a big, positive difference in my financials when I had new member one-time fees. If you have to, reduce it, but don't waive it.

Leave of Absence (LOA)

A leave of absence is when a member needs to temporarily put their membership on hold due to not being able to make the meetings for some period of time due to an unforeseen circumstance. They expect to return to the group and aren't asking to terminate their membership. What they're asking for is permission to miss *X* number of meetings, and they don't want to pay for meetings they're going to miss. Examples of legitimate LOA reasons are massive projects, like acquisitions, overseas travel for extended periods, sickness, or some combination of situations like conferences or extended family vacations. The key is that the LOA isn't a substitute for someone not prioritizing the meetings on their calendar or making up for their poor planning and not wanting to pay for a missed meeting. It's the exception to the rule.

Questions to Ask Yourself

What will be an acceptable leave of absence time frame: three months, four months? When is an LOA acceptable? Should the members vote on another member's LOA request? Will I charge zero or reduced dues during the LOA? How will I keep the member engaged during their LOA? How will the member reenter the group after their LOA? Can they participate virtually instead of LOA, and if so, is that an option for the group and them? Will the member really return, and is there a date to do so? Do I want to retain the member?

Better Practices

Ideally, an LOA is three or four months. Any longer, and the member is disconnected from the group and probably not returning. Furthermore, the group has started to forget about them. I recommend reducing the membership fee but not to zero. Choose an amount, usually 25 percent of the total dues, to hold the member's seat at the table until they return. In exchange for that 25 percent, they also remain on all communication, you still do their QAS, and they have access to all the other benefits that go with membership, like reaching out to you or other members between meetings. It's also a great practice to assign an existing member to reach out to them monthly to check in. This tactic alone practically ensures the LOA member's return.

Should I Offer a Guarantee?

Offering a guarantee should be a benefit to you and the prospect. Otherwise, don't do it. What constitutes a guarantee? It supports your belief that whatever your offering (the MX) is so compelling you guarantee they'll have that level of experience (e.g., exquisite, excellent, satisfied customer … *choose your words carefully and define them*). And if they don't, they get their money back.

 Questions to Ask Yourself

Will offering a guarantee help me grow faster and close my ideal member prospects? How often might I have to honor the guarantee? Is my guarantee, if I offer one, compelling enough to matter? How much is my guarantee? What conditions have to be met to qualify for the guarantee? Have I spelled out exactly what I'm guaranteeing?

 Better Practices

For years, I've offered a one-month membership guarantee. If a new member didn't like their first meeting, I would refund that meeting's dues. And I've never had a member take me up on it. Not once. *Why?* Because I also have them commit mentally for three months, and the value they receive in onboarding and the first meeting is exceptional beyond their expectations. So why offer the guarantee? Because it gives those prospects who've never participated in a PaC the comfort of knowing they have nothing to lose. It handles the objection: *I want to sit in a group before deciding.* No need to; you have a guarantee. They still pay for onboarding because there's value for them in the process regardless, so that's not refunded. It also sends a message that you believe in the value for them so much that you're putting your money behind it. I put it on every application as a standard offering.

Should I Pay for Referrals and Kickbacks?

Getting referrals validates the work you do, plus they're fun to receive. Who doesn't like to call a referral? The questions are: Do you pay your members for referrals, incentivize them in some way? And do you also take a fee from those you refer business to? This comes into play when you're acting as a Resource Connector. Your member may ask to be referred to someone, and when you refer, do you expect to get a referral fee?

 Questions to Ask Yourself

Will incentivizing my members for referrals make a difference? Do they want to be incentivized? Should I pay centers of influence, family, friends, etc. for referring a member to me? Should I take a fee for referring my members to a vendor? Will it look like I'm biased? When is it appropriate (if at all) for me to take a fee?

 Better Practices

This is a personal decision on both fronts. I've never taken a fee from a vendor because I've wanted to be neutral, and I always recommend more than one vendor so the member has a choice. But there are circumstances where receiving a fee is common and acceptable. Again, it's up to you. Regarding paying for referrals, I've tried monetary payments to members, donations to the charity of their choice, paying-it-forward monetary awards, and nothing. The bottom line is that I found it didn't really matter. The members referred because they wanted to; it's like a club to them. They're honored to refer a right-fit prospect because they're proud of being a member of your group—*their* group. In fact, when I offered anything monetary, they were offended. So I write a thank-you note instead!

PS: You can offer the referred prospect a discount for month one because they were referred. That makes the referee look good and the prospect feel special.

Succession or Wind-Down?

What's your vision for how long you'll be moderating PaCs? What happens when you want to slow down, quit, or retire? Your members are relying on you to keep going; they don't think about what occurs if something happens to you. They expect the group to continue indefinitely. So having a plan isn't just for you; it's for them too.

 ### Questions to Ask Yourself

Do I want a payday for all my efforts in starting and retaining groups? Do my members want to keep meeting? Are my members ready for a change to elevate their MX? Do I want to manage a team of moderators running my groups? Have I been doing this long enough to have consistent stats on retention, member dues, etc.? Do I want to stay involved but not run the meetings?

 ### Better Practices

This is a personal decision, but make it with you *and* your members in mind. Don't choose wind-down if your group will be thriving or is thriving when you want to leave. As a responsible moderator, you won't be able to just let the group go, fall apart, or stop if the members really want to continue. I've never seen a wind-down that's effectively executed. Either the moderator is moderating past their time and the members are staying because they feel obligated to, or they think retirement is coming. Succession is a plan. When properly executed, it's where you mentor someone to take over your groups for a minimum of ninety days, and you pay them a percentage of the revenues, or they pay you outright for the group (i.e., it's an acquisition). The members are involved in the transition by approving the new moderator or being involved in the details of the transition.

Other Decisions to Make at Some Point (Some Sooner Rather Than Later, Depending on Your Situation)

- **What method will you use to track prospects and member data?** An Excel sheet, Google Docs, or a more advanced method, such as a CRM (customer relationship management) system?
- **Will you have administrative help, or won't it be needed?** If so, will you outsource, use a virtual assistant, or use someone geographically close to you because you want to meet in person or have them attend in-person meetings to help set up?
- **If you have speakers, will you pay them or expect them to speak gratis?**
- **Do you want to do consulting for your members, and if so, do you have types of consulting you will and won't do?** For example: You facilitate leadership meetings, strategic planning sessions, succession planning, or whatever your area of expertise is.
- **What assessments might you want to be certified in and offer?** Assessments like DiSC, Kolbe, and Predictive Index are a few to consider that can enhance the MX and give you as a moderator insight into what they need as members of a group.

- **Company entity.** Do you have an established company? If not, establish one as you need a firewall between you personally and professionally. Also, it shows you're serious about this as a business.

- **Company name.** Have a name that says what you do. Consider a tagline that describes it, and then try to secure a domain for your website and email address if you want to go that route.

- **Group name.** What will you call your PaCs? "Bob's PaCs" isn't ideal, but whatever the name, it should say what you do and who the group caters to.

- **Domain name.** Explore buying your business name domain name, if available, to protect yourself and also buy your name as a domain, as well (e.g., Tinacornerstolz.com).

- **Will you have a website, and if so, how will it promote your PaCs?** If you have an existing website, how will you incorporate PaCs into it?

- **Will you have an email address that has a company URL?** Not Gmail.

- **Get insured.** Get personal liability insurance to protect yourself and commercial liability insurance if you're doing consulting. Many companies will require this to do business with you.

- **Business cards.** Today there are digital business card options as well as physical cards. Decide if you need or want business cards and, if so, what type.

Research has shown that adults make at least thirty-five thousand decisions a day.[11] While there are not thirty-five thousand decisions here for you to make about your PaC business, there are probably close to one hundred questions for you to answer. Take your time now to establish a solid foundation. Thoughtfully decide what's best for you before beginning to market your PaC business. If you do this, I guarantee you'll have more confidence and more success immediately.

Takeaways

- Take time to do the hard work now for the decisions you haven't made yet.
- Align your decisions with your choice of type of peer group, level, and delivery method.

Resources

- Access the Decision Checklist using the QR code at the back of the book.

---

11   Heidi Zak, "Adults Make More than 35,000 Decisions per Day. Here Are 4 Ways to Prevent Mental Burnout," https://www.inc.com/ (Inc.), accessed November 17, 2022, https://www.inc.com/heidi-zak/adults-make-more-than-35000-decisions-per-day-here-are-4-ways-to-prevent-mental-burnout.html.

CONCLUSION

Final Insights

In chapter 1, I described my experience at the French Laundry. Fine dining has so much in common with owning a peer advisory council business and moderating its meetings. *Do you see it now?* Every decision made affects the customer, whether that person is a diner or a member of your PaC. You're creating a member experience (MX) around the needs of your customers—your members. From choosing your area of focus to whether you will be virtual or in person, and every decision thereafter, you're the architect of the experiences of the dozen members in the room. Who will get along like magic with whom? Which eager prospect isn't a good fit for a group, so you'll have to pass on them for now?

The topic I haven't gotten into yet is love. In March of 2022, Sally Schmitt, the founder of the French Laundry (she sold it to chef Thomas Keller in 1994) passed away at ninety years old. In her book *Six California Kitchens: A Collection of Recipes, Stories, and Cooking Lessons from a Pioneer of California Cuisine*, she wrote, "I really have done just what I loved to do, which has always been simply to cook good food for those I cared for. ... That's what mattered. That's all that mattered."

People who succeed at the business of PaCs and moderating them do so because they love what they're doing. They have a deep care and concern for their members, and they always put them first. They love the category they work in, because trust me, if they didn't, it would show. This is a business that has so much care woven into it. It prioritizes the members, and it does everything possible to improve the odds of their success. It takes selflessness and commitment to getting members to see the value in the group and to notice when their own insights are developing.

Meanwhile, all the care and concern in the world won't make up for a meeting that has no grounding or direction. Moderators must also have a love of structure as well as a feel for when it should be held lightly. I know that idea can seem daunting. Here I am, presenting you with all of this structure and these guidelines and lists, and then I say: know all of this, but if you really know what you're doing, you'll know when to leave things out or switch them around.

The advice I'll leave you with, after all of this talk of doing things in the service of an exquisite MX, is to sit with all of this for a moment. Remember the journey from unconscious incompetence to unconscious competence? The latter is like a flow state, in which you're not even thinking about what you're doing or why. Instead, the best move for the members in the room simply occurs to you as your default. That's likely a ways down the road, but you'll never get there if you don't start.

So start, but start smart, meaning you should take a moment to allow the information in this book to sink in. Make a plan, and choose Strategic Partners. Or if you're already running groups, where are you on the Journey Map? What is your next step on the Journey Map?

Make a plan for taking that step. And as I suggest, don't move too quickly through the process. Be thorough rather than fast. Backpedaling is expensive and time consuming and sometimes embarrassing. Try things on first.

I'm a fast mover and high achiever, and I wish someone had told me to slow down and savor being thorough and measured over starting groups faster and with a bang. You have the benefit of learning from not just my mistakes and successes here but also the mistakes and successes of the people who've gone through my academy. Follow the processes in this book, giving yourself space and time to be certain about crucial decisions like your category, your pricing, and your MX. You'll sleep better and be more confident with your groups when you know you've made all the right decisions for the right reasons.

Once you've done all that, you might be surprised by how calm you can be. When you feel—from the inside out—the security that comes with knowing you dotted all your i's, you have a different energy. You come across differently: not harried and always catching up but centered, grounded, and looking ahead. And this energy increases with time. You get very comfortable in your own skin.

Seasoned moderators are able to deliver exquisite member experiences, not because they've got the best processes but because of the wisdom they've acquired that informs everything they do. My wish for you is that you stick it out through all of the mishaps and mistakes, and the starts and stops and restarts, and get to that place of wisdom. What's the best way to do that? Find a mentor or a set of peers yourself.

My mentor in this industry was Arthur Sharff. Very sadly, Arthur passed as I was writing this conclusion. Arthur got involved in the industry when it was just taking off in the late '70s after participating in groups himself when he owned his own paper company. His early involvement shaped the global Young Presidents' Organization (YPO) moderator training program. He codeveloped it. Arthur taught me all about the skills of moderating—including the importance of being silent and the reasons for being selfless. He was my biggest cheerleader.

Arthur had a trademark move I'd like to share: pebbles. Arthur always carried pebbles in his pocket. He was always ready to share his wisdom, and when he did, he handed you a pebble to pass it forward. If you shared wisdom with him, he gave you a pebble as well. They were of different colors and shapes, and they were always smooth and shiny, just like his wisdom.

> *Drop a pebble in the water, just a splash and it's gone. But there are half a hundred ripples circling on and on and on. Ever spreading from the center flowing on out to the sea. And there is no way of telling where the end is going to be ...*
>
> —JAMES W. FOLEY

By running peer groups, you're watching over your members as they share their pebbles with each other, pebbles that will make a ripple effect beyond the meeting room. Sometimes you add your own. And you might even get some. Know that a man named Arthur paved your way because he paved mine. And pay it forward. Help someone else become a great moderator of peer groups!

Finally, enjoy yourself! There's no use being in this business unless you're having fun, enjoying the people you work with, and loving it.

WANT TO START
YOUR JOURNEY NOW?

Visit tinacornerstolz.com/resources and see how you can:

1. Access **free training** to get started with understanding the peer group industry or to be a better moderator.

2. Join our **community** to be with other peers who are interested in or already leading peer groups.

3. Use this QR code to download all the free **resources** mentioned in this book:

4. Explore whether you're ready for our **Peer Advisory Council Academy**.

5. Receive a pebble. Send a note to me at info@tinacornerstolz. com with your address and your favorite words of wisdom, and I'll send you a special pebble along with Arthur's PowerPoint of "pebbles"—words of wisdom he gave to his President's Council members.

ABOUT THE AUTHOR

Tina Corner-Stolz unleashed the secret of the power of peer groups in *Sit Down! Speak Up! Cash In!: A CEO's Guide to Peer Advisory Groups*, and she's back with a how-to for creating a lucrative business by moderating peer advisory councils (PaCs) in *Your Seat at the Table*.

Over a decade ago, Tina cracked the code of the peer group industry with the most successful start-up franchise sold at the highest multiple ever recorded. She accumulated over twenty thousand hours creating, developing, and moderating lucrative peer advisory councils and mentoring others to do so through her Peer Advisory Council Academy.

Tina found that the key to successful peer advisory councils is an exquisite member experience (MX), created by a skillful moderator. In this book you'll learn what that means and follow Tina as she guides you, step-by-step, through identifying your PaC's theme, assembling it, and moderating it so it stays together for years because of the value the members get from their experience.

Tina is a graduate of the University of Missouri, INSEAD, and Harvard executive programs. She and her husband, Scott, split their time between Saint Petersburg, Florida, and the Lake of the Ozarks.